KU-470-165

A SHORT HISTO
OF THE
EPISCOPAL CHURCH IN SCOTLAND

A SHORT HISTORY OF THE EPISCOPAL CHURCH IN SCOTLAND

FROM THE RESTORATION TO THE PRESENT TIME

FREDERICK GOLDIE

Bishop of Glasgow and Galloway

THE SAINT ANDREW PRESS
EDINBURGH

This edition first published in 1976 by
THE SAINT ANDREW PRESS
121 George Street, Edinburgh

First edition (S.P.C.K.) 1951
Second edition   1976

© Frederick Goldie 1976

ISBN 0 7152 0315 0

PRINTED IN GREAT BRITAIN BY
R. & R. CLARK LTD, EDINBURGH

CONTENTS

ACKNOWLEDGEMENTS

Acknowledgements are due to James Clarke and Co., Ltd., for permission to quote from Dr. Archibald Main's Foreword to *Robert Leighton* by Bp. E. Knox, and to David Winter and Son, Ltd., for permission to quote from a paper by Canon J. A. MacCulloch published in successive issues of the *Scottish Guardian*, February—April 1949.

FOREWORD

By the Most Reverend Richard K. Wimbush
*Bishop of Argyll and The Isles, and Primus
of the Episcopal Church in Scotland*

THE call for a second enlarged edition of Bishop Goldie's history nearly a quarter of a century after its first appearance proves the enduring value of this work and the reliability of its record of the history of the Scottish Episcopal Church. Nowhere else are the facts readily available within the compass of a single volume. In these days when progress in ecumenical understanding is an essential precursor to closer executive or organic association, each branch of the Church in Scotland should try to present an honest and fair account of its own life, for the use of its own members and also for the information of other Churches within and beyond Scotland.

Since the Second World War the Episcopal Church has widened its horizons. It has sought to play a significant part in the Anglican world, far and wide, and in the increased intercourse between the Churches of Christendom, Roman Catholic, Orthodox and Protestant—partly through direct dialogue, partly through the Councils of the Churches. Bishop Goldie has played a quiet yet active part in this development. The new edition of his book brings the record up to date, completing the history of the Episcopal Church up to the mid-seventies.

†RICHARD ARGYLL AND THE ISLES
Primus

PREFACE

In tracing the story of the Episcopal Church in Scotland from the Restoration of 1660 to the middle of the twentieth century, my purpose has been to assist churchmen in understanding the native traditions which have been woven into the developing life of the Church in the light of the history of the past three centuries.

History has been described as " a cordial for drooping spirits ". Faced with the great problems of the middle years of the twentieth century, many might be disposed to grow weary and faint-hearted. I trust this volume will assist meditations on the survival and growth of the Church through difficulties and hazards far more intense than any of the present time, and that the inheritors of the labours of churchmen of former days may rise from these meditations to press on with the work waiting to be done.

. " Seeing we are compassed about with so great a cloud of witnesses, let us also lay aside every weight, and the sin which doth so easily beset us, and let us run with patience the race that is set before us, looking unto Jesus the author and perfecter of our faith."

F. GOLDIE

NOTE TO SECOND EDITION

For reasons of economy the text of the first ten chapters has been left very much as in the first edition. Chapter 11 has been slightly revised and a new Chapter 12 added to bring the account to the present day—1975.

A BRIEF ACCOUNT OF THE HISTORY OF THE CHURCH IN SCOTLAND FROM THE REFORMATION (1560) TO THE RESTORATION (1660)

IN the chaos which fell upon the Church of Scotland after the tumultuous Reformation of 1560, the old hierarchy became extinct. The Archbishop of St. Andrews was put to death in 1571. The Archbishop of Glasgow fled to Paris and lived in exile there till his death in 1603. Several Bishops openly joined the Reformers and continued to exercise jurisdiction in their dioceses, but no attempt was made to continue the episcopal succession.[1]

In spite of the plan outlined in the First Book of Discipline, the land which had been taken from the old Church by the nobles was not returned to the new Church, and financial problems became very troublesome. Besides, the Reformation Settlement, which was neither Episcopal nor Presbyterian, was not working very well. In these circumstances a Convention was summoned at Leith in January 1572.[2] The preacher of the

[1] The Bishops of Galloway, Orkney, and Caithness were given commissions by the General Assembly (June 25th, 1563) to plant churches within the bounds of their dioceses (Peterkin, *Booke of the Universal Kirk of Scotland*, p. 14; Calderwood, *History of the Kirk of Scotland*, vol. 2, p. 223). The Queen, Mary, did her utmost to break the Reformation Settlement and to seek the continuity of the Episcopal Succession. John Sinclair, chosen by the Queen to celebrate her marriage with Darnley, was appointed to the see of Brechin in 1565, and John Leslie, a strong defender of the hierarchy, was nominated to the see of Ross, probably in the same year. It seems certain that the Queen's intention was to secure support for her design to restore the Church to the Roman obedience (J. Knox, *History of the Reformation of the Church in Scotland*, vol. 1, p. 265, vol. 2, pp. 398, 600; Keith, *History of the Affairs of Church and State in Scotland*, pp. 165, 194, 198-200). Queen Mary was obliged to abdicate during her imprisonment at Lochleven, and the infant prince was crowned and anointed by the Bishop of Orkney.

[2] Calderwood, vol. 3, pp. 168-196; Grub, *Ecclesiastical History of Scotland*, vol. 2, pp. 176-181.

opening sermon of the Convention spoke of " the foul deformity and desolation of your churches and temples, which are more like sheep cots than the house of God ", and said of the ministers of the word that " they are utterly neglected ".   It was agreed at Leith to establish a " titular " Episcopacy in Scotland following the pattern of the pre-Reformation Church and that the Bishops should be consecrated, though no provision was made for a legitimate consecration.   Those who were expected to lay hands on the Bishops had not themselves been consecrated.   Further, it was declared that the Bishops should have no greater jurisdiction than was already possessed by superintendents, but should be subject to the General Assemblies of the Church in spiritual matters.[1]   Soon afterwards, John Douglas, Rector of the University of St. Andrews, was " consecrated " Archbishop of St. Andrews, and vacancies at Glasgow, Dunkeld, Dunblane, and Moray were filled by other titular Bishops.

During these years, the General Assembly continued to meet and to superintend the affairs of the whole Church and the conduct of all orders of the clergy.   The Minister of Dunfermline was elected Moderator in 1573; the Bishop of Glasgow in 1575.   The leader of the Presbyterians, Andrew Melville, became Moderator in 1578 and led the Assembly to a decision that no more vacant Bishoprics should for the present be filled, and that the Bishops already appointed should minister to one flock only and should not usurp any other jurisdiction, or vote in

[1] The titular Bishops are frequently called " tulchan Bishops ".   A tulchan was a calf's skin stuffed with straw and set up beside a cow to encourage her to yield her milk.   It was said of these Bishops that they were " tulchans " because they were appointed by patrons who reserved to themselves the chief revenues of the sees.   Dean Mowat (*Scottish Church History*, p. 96) calls the titular Bishops " mock Bishops ", and adds, " The mock Bishops of this period swell the list of the ruffians of the Reformation ".   Grub, vol. 2, p. 225, writes of " tulchan Bishops " thus: " That epithet has erroneously, or with an intentional disregard of facts, been connected by many writers with the titular episcopacy established at Leith.   Nominations of that kind had been made previous to the agreement at Leith, and they continued to take place after Melville had succeeded in overturning it."

Parliament in the name of the Church. Melville's scheme for the reform of church government was approved by the General Assembly of 1581, when it accepted the Second Book of Discipline, which aimed at creating a hierarchy of ecclesiastical courts, the Kirk Session in each congregation, the Presbytery in each district, the Synod in each province, and the General Assembly for the nation.[1]   The Privy Council refused to ratify the Second Book of Discipline, and King James vigorously opposed the setting up of ecclesiastical courts and was determined to disallow their jurisdiction.   In an effort to enforce their scheme, Melville and fellow Commissioners of the General Assembly took part in " The Raid of Ruthven ", secured the person of James, and imprisoned him in Stirling Castle.   The General Assembly expressed its disapproval of the violence, but proceeded to establish Presbyterianism.

However, the King escaped from confinement and summoned Parliament, which, in 1584, passed what Presbyterians call " The Black Acts ".[2]   These Acts established the authority of the King over all causes civil and ecclesiastical, subjected the clergy to the authority of the secular courts, and enacted that all convocations must have the royal licence and that the Bishops should have the jurisdiction of the Church.

A temporary triumph for Melville followed the repeal of the Acts of 1584 by the Parliament of 1592,[3] but the aversion to Presbyterianism which King James expressed so clearly in his

---

[1] The titular Archbishop Adamson of St. Andrews vigorously opposed the policy of Melville and the Presbyterians.   In 1584 he published a summary of his principles in which he claimed apostolic institution for the office of Bishop, and declared that Episcopacy is most agreeable to the primitive Church, that ordination and government belong to the Bishops, and that Presbyteries do little else but create confusion and sedition in the Church (Calderwood, vol. 4, pp. 49–55, 157–167; Grub, vol. 2, pp. 232–234).

[2] *Acts P.S.*, vol. 3, pp. 290–312.

[3] Ib., pp. 541, 542.   The Act of 1592 virtually established Presbyterianism in Scotland for the first time, but the opposition of the King and the growing strength of the titular Bishops made the Presbyterian triumph only temporary (Calderwood, vol. 5, pp. 156–166; *James Melville's Diary*, pp. 294–298).

Basilikon Doron (1599) guided him in a series of steps which led to the beginning of the First Canonical Episcopacy in 1610. The *Basilikon Doron* was a book of directions on government, addressed to Prince Henry, his son. In it, James advocated the supremacy of the King in matters ecclesiastical and showed the inconsistency of Presbyterian parity with a monarchy and the necessity of Episcopacy for the well-being of Church and State, saying that Puritans were " very pests in the Church and commonweal ".[1] Later, when he became King of England, he declared at the Hampton Court Conference: " A Scottish Presbytery as well agreeth with a monarchy as God and the devil."

A General Assembly was held at Glasgow under the presidency of the titular Archbishop of Glasgow in 1610.[2] Thirteen Bishops, thirteen noblemen, and more than a hundred ministers were present. This Assembly agreed that the right of ordination and discipline should rest in the hands of the Bishops, that all incumbents should take an oath of obedience to the King and Bishop on admission, and that patrons must present their candidates for benefices to the Bishop, who, after trial and examination of the presentee, would arrange the ordination or induction. These decisions established the authority of the Episcopate once more in Scotland; it now remained to secure for the titular Bishops valid consecration.[3] The consecration took place in

[1] *Basilikon Doron*, bk. 2, p. 160: " I protest before the great God that ye shall never find with any Highland or border thieves greater ingratitude and more lies, and vile perjuries, than with these fanatic spirits."

[2] King James appointed men to vacant Bishoprics after 1592 when Presbyterianism was virtually established, and by a series of adroit political steps succeeded in strengthening the power and influence of these titular Bishops (Calderwood, vol. 4, pp. 96–100; Spottiswood, *History of the Church of Scotland*, vol. 3, pp. 84–90). His plan to restore Episcopacy in Scotland was even more vigorously pursued after his succession to the throne of England in 1603. On the death of Archbishop Beaton, he appointed John Spottiswood to the see of Glasgow on July 20th, 1603, and found in the new Archbishop a most vigorous supporter of his measures for the re-establishment of the hierarchy in Scotland (Spottiswood, vol. 3, p. 140; Russell, " Life of Spottiswood ").

[3] Calderwood, vol. 7, pp. 91–103; Cook, *History of the Church of Scotland*, vol. 2, pp. 227–237. Grub, vol. 2, p. 294, writes: " When the proceedings were over, a sum of five thousand pounds Scots was distributed by the Earl of

London on October 21st, 1610. Archbishop Spottiswood of Glasgow, Bishop Hamilton of Galloway, and Bishop Lamb of Brechin were consecrated *per saltum* by the Bishops of London, Ely, Rochester, and Worcester.[1] On their return to Scotland, the newly consecrated Bishops consecrated to the Episcopate their brethren who occupied the other sees.

The General Assembly at Perth in 1618 agreed to Five Articles concerning worship and the rites of the Church. The first article prescribed that the Blessed Sacrament should be received by the people, not sitting, but " meekly and reverently upon their knees ". The second permitted private Communion for the sick. The third permitted private Baptism and enjoined immediate Baptism. The fourth provided for Confirmation by the Bishop, and the fifth restored the observance of the principal Festivals of the Christian Year.[2]

With Archbishop Laud as his adviser, Charles I determined to speed up the policy of his father. He asserted his royal right to prescribe the ceremonies of the Church and the robes of the clergy, and issued through the Privy Council " An Act anent the Service Book " to ensure that the new service book in preparation be used in every parish.[3] When the new service book was published in 1637, though it bore the marks of the labours of the Scottish Bishops Maxwell and Wedderburn, there was organized opposition to its use because of the manner of its introduction. Several riots took place in Edinburgh as a protest

---

Dunbar among those ministers who had acted as moderators of presbyteries. The opponents of the Synod asserted that the money was given to secure the votes of the members. There can be little doubt that its distribution was entrusted to the earl for the purpose, at least, of rewarding the ministers who supported the measures recommended by the Sovereign."

[1] On the day of the consecration, one who was present wrote in his diary: " This Lord's day, by God's blessing, was not ill spent. For I was invited to be present at the consecration of two bishops and an archbishop of Scotland. I witnessed that ceremony, and the imposition of hands, and the whole service. O God, how great was my delight " (Isaac Casaubon, quoted by Calderwood, vol. 7, p. 151).

[2] Grub, vol. 2, pp. 314–319; Lindsay, *Perth Assembly*, pp. 19–72; Spottiswood, vol. 3, pp. 252–257.   [3] Grub, vol. 2, p. 374.

against the introduction of the Liturgy, but it seems probable that the riots were engineered.[1] A group of ministers, led by Alexander Henderson, the minister at Leuchars in Fife, presented a petition against the Prayer Book to the Privy Council on the grounds that the book had not the warrant of either General Assembly or Parliament, and that since the Church of Scotland was a free and independent Church its pastors were best able to provide what was for the good of the people. The King again ordered that the book be read and that all who had helped in the riots be punished.

Out of this situation the National Uprising in Scotland developed. Many patriots felt that Scotland was being treated as a mere satellite of England. There was a powerful sense of impatience at the interference of Charles I in Scottish affairs. Nobles and landlords were particularly concerned to encourage opposition against the King on account of the Act of Revocation by which the King revoked all grants of church lands since 1540 and thus attempted to make better provision for the stipends of the clergy.

The uprising, which had been gathering momentum during the closing months of 1637, reached a high pitch of excitement in certain quarters when the National Covenant was drawn up and signed

---

[1] On the occasion of the uproar in St. Giles, the Archbishop of St. Andrews, the Archbishop of Glasgow, the Bishop of Edinburgh, and several other Bishops were present in the church. When Dr. Hanna, Dean of Edinburgh, began the service there was so much noise and confusion that the prayers could not be heard. The Bishop of Edinburgh was also interrupted when he addressed the congregation from the pulpit, and in the course of his address a stool was thrown at him. The rioters were thrust out of the church by the magistrates who were present and the service continued (Grub, vol. 2, pp. 384–386; Gordon, *Scots Affairs*, vol. 1, pp. 7–12; Rothes, *Relation of Proceedings,* Appendix, pp. 198–200). Bishop Mitchell, *Scotland's Church*, p. 86, writes: "Organised riots took place in other churches, but that of St. Giles has been made historic by the name of the mythical Jenny Geddes. The only person of that name known to contemporary historians was a Jenet Geddes who showed her loyalty to Charles II at the Restoration of 1661 around the bonfires in the High Street of Edinburgh. Yet a modern tablet in St. Giles' marks the spot from which (so visitors are told) she hurled her legendary stool, which also, for the acceptance of the credulous, may be seen in the antiquarian museum of Edinburgh."

in Edinburgh and other towns.[1] The purpose of the Covenant was to bind subscribers to resist any innovations in the worship or government of the Church until they had been approved in a free General Assembly and Parliament. However, there was strong opposition to the " National Covenant ", as it is commonly called. The Universities of St. Andrews and Aberdeen formally condemned it, and the Aberdeen Doctors described it as illegal, disloyal, and implying a breach from the rest of Protestantism and the ancient Church.[2]

The General Assembly which met at Glasgow in November 1638 was carefully prepared for by the Covenanters.[3] None of the Bishops were present. Only one hundred and forty ministers attended, and these chiefly from the lowlands of Scotland. The Commissioner tried to close the proceedings when he saw that every decision of the Assembly seemed to be directed against the King's will. However, the Assembly continued their deliberations and condemned the six previous Assemblies of 1606, 1608, 1610, 1616, 1617, and 1618; they deposed all Bishops, abjured Episcopacy, condemned the service book and ordinal, and restored the Presbyterian church courts.[4]

The next decade is one of intermittent civil war and confusion. The armies of the Covenanters were everywhere victorious in battle, or were unopposed. When the Long Parliament in England began its work the Scottish Covenanters readily agreed to give their support, as defined in the Solemn League and

---

[1] Rothes, pp. 70–79; Kerr, *The Covenants and the Covenanters*; Gordon, *Scots Affairs*, vol. 1, pp. 63–80.

[2] Grub, vol. 3, pp. 12–16; Gordon, *Scots Affairs*, vol. 1, pp. 82–96; Garden, " Life of Dr. John Forbes ", pp. 35–40.

[3] The Covenanters, determined on the policy of slandering the supporters of the Church, and in particular the Bishops, proceeded to put forward charges of shameful immoralities, which they could not prove. Balcanqual (*Large Declaration*, pp. 230–232) says: " This now is that libel with which the Covenanters did undoubtedly compass their own end, which was to raise up in the people an utter abhorring of the present bishops' persons and calling, but with what religion, justice or honesty, they have effected it, others besides themselves, both in heaven and earth, must judge and give sentence."

[4] Grub, vol. 3, pp. 32–49; Peterkin, pp. 26–42, 163–193; Gordon, *Scots Affairs*, vol. 2, pp. 97–101, 131–175.

Covenant of 1643. The purpose of the agreement was to unite England and Scotland in an engagement to preserve the rights and liberties of Parliament, to preserve the Reformed religion in Scotland, and to reform religion in England and Ireland in doctrine, worship, discipline, and government " according to the Word of God and the examples of the best reformed churches ".[1] It has been said that the National Covenant united, but the Solemn League and Covenant divided, the Church in Scotland. At any rate, the Marquis of Montrose, who had taken a leading part in the victories of the Covenanters after 1638, now became leader of a royalist army. The cruelty of the Covenanters in this period is a grim and terrible story, notably in the way the followers of the defeated Montrose were executed after the battle of Philiphaugh.[2]

After the betrayal of Charles I in 1647 and his execution in 1649, there appeared a number of divisions amongst the Covenanters and moderate Presbyterians. During the seven years (1653–1660) of General Monk's dictatorship in Scotland, however, the General Assembly was silenced, and religious sects developed at a rate unknown in the former history of Scotland.

In these troubles which fell upon the Church in Scotland in the years subsequent to the publication of the " National Covenant " of 1638, the line of Bishops from the consecration in Westminster Abbey of 1610 became almost exterminated. The domination of Cromwell—following upon the signing of the " National Covenant ", the Civil Wars, and the murder of Charles I—made it difficult to continue the line of episcopal succession. One Bishop alone remained, Dr. Thomas Sydserff, Bishop of Galloway, and he, in advanced years, was translated to the Bishopric of Orkney soon after the Restoration.[3]

---

[1] Baillie, *Letters and Journals*, vol. 2, pp. 99–250; Peterkin, pp. 400–404, 416–434.　　　　　　　　　　　　　　　　　[2] John Buchan, *Montrose*.

[3] Bishop Sydserff probably resided in France during most of the Commonwealth period. In 1650 he ordained Durell and Brevint, afterwards Deans of Windsor and Durham, in Paris (*Evelyn's Diary*, vol. 1, p. 258). He also ordained John Tillotson, afterwards Archbishop of Canterbury (*Pepys's Diary*, vol. 1, p. 242).

2

A GENERAL PICTURE OF THE ESTABLISHED EPISCOPAL CHURCH IN SCOTLAND DURING THE RESTORATION PERIOD (1660–1688)

The Restoration and the Act Rescissory

AT the Restoration in 1660 steps were taken to restore the Church. There is good reason to believe that the restoration of the Church as constituted in the days of James I and Charles I was welcomed in Scotland. A leader of the Presbyterian party, Robert Douglas,[1] who was greatly concerned lest Episcopacy should be restored, wrote: " The generality of this new upstart generation h've no love for Presbyterial government, but are wearied of 'hat yoke, feeding themselves with the fancy of Episcopacy or moderate Episcopacy."

The Scottish Parliament which met in 1661 was resolved to acknowledge the royal authority clearly. It ordered that all Members of Parliament and all persons holding offices of state should take the oath of allegiance, acknowledging His Majesty to be supreme governor of the kingdom over all persons and in all causes, and promising never to decline his jurisdiction. The Solemn League and Covenant was declared to be no longer binding, and the violent proceedings during the rebellion were condemned. Later, the Acts passed in the Parliaments from 1640 to 1648 were rescinded and annulled. The King then

---

[1] Minister successively at Kirkcaldy and Edinburgh, a leader of the Covenanters. He expressed his regret that " a generation had risen in Scotland disposed to condemn even the Covenant itself, to which they bore a heart hatred ". A series of letters passed between Sharp and Douglas which give a vivid account of the ecclesiastical proceedings of the time (Wodrow, *History of the Sufferings of the Church of Scotland*, vol. 1, pp. 4–54)

declared his resolution to maintain the true Reformed Protestant religion in its purity of doctrine and worship as it was established under his royal father and grandfather. The Act Rescissory, in abolishing the Presbyterian form of government, empowered the King to settle the ecclesiastical polity of Scotland.[1] His Majesty announced his intention of restoring Episcopacy, and in a letter which was laid before the Privy Council and received the assent of their general satisfaction, he declared that, on account of the unsuitableness of the late form of ecclesiastical polity to the monarchical estate and on account of the violence done during the troubles to the royal prerogative and the civil and ecclesiastical government, and for the Glory of God, the interest of the Protestant religion, the order, peace and unity of the Church, and its better harmony with the ecclesiastical government in England and Ireland, it was his resolution to restore the Church to its right government by Bishops, as it was by law before the late troubles began, and as it now stood settled by law.

Most of the Synods in the southern half of Scotland were unfavourable to the re-establishment of Episcopacy, but north of the Tay no remonstrances were made against the ecclesiastical changes.[2] The Synod of Aberdeen unanimously agreed to send an address to the Commissioners and the High Court of Parliament expressing their deep sorrow and regret for the national guilt and requesting that His Majesty be petitioned to settle the ecclesiastical government according to the word of God and the practice of the ancient primitive Church, in such a way as might be most consistent with the royal authority and most conducive to godliness, unity, peace, and order.[3] There seems no doubt that the majority of the ministers of the diocese of Aberdeen

---

[1] *Acts P.S.*, vol. 7, pp. 3–367, and Appendix, pp. 59, 78–81.
[2] Wodrow, *History*, vol. 1, pp. 109–130; Grub, vol. 3, pp. 178–181.
[3] A complete copy of the " flattering address in favour of Episcopacy ", as Wodrow describes it, with names of the signatories of the Synod of Edinburgh, is preserved amongst the Papers of the Episcopal Church in Scotland in the Theological College, Edinburgh.

preferred Episcopacy and strongly disliked the rebellious courses which had so long prevailed. They therefore welcomed the re-establishment of the ancient ecclesiastical polity.

The Scottish Bishops of the Second English Consecration

Now that the restoration of the Episcopal Church was determined by the Government, a new consecration of Bishops was necessary, since Bishop Sydserff, formerly of Galloway, was the only survivor of the old Episcopate. The persons selected for the episcopal office, to be consecrated in London, were James Sharp for the Archbishopric of St. Andrews, Andrew Fairfoull for the Archbishopric of Glasgow, James Hamilton for Galloway, and Robert Leighton for Dunblane.

James Sharp has been denounced by the Presbyterians as a traitor and as one of the most odious and cruel of men. His supporters described him as a man of great abilities and personal virtues. He was born in Banff and baptized by the incumbent there in 1618. He graduated at Aberdeen, and then for a time resided in England, where he was during the turmoils of the Covenant in 1638. Later he returned to Scotland as a Professor at St. Andrews. In 1648 he was inducted as minister of Crail in Fife. Having distinguished himself as a leader of the Resolutioners, a moderate party of Presbyterians, Sharp was chosen as their deputy at London and at Breda. He spent several months in London in 1660, and was much in the company of General Monk, Scottish nobles, Episcopal clergy, and Presbyterian ministers there, and during this period he visited Charles at Breda and was appointed Chaplain to the King for Scotland.[1] The Resolutioners intimated to Charles at Breda that they were " no enemies to moderate Episcopacy ".

Andrew Fairfoull is described by Presbyterians as " possessed of considerable learning; better skilled, however, in physic

---

[1] Keith, *Historical Catalogue of the Scottish Bishops*, pp. 41, 42; Lyon, *History of St. Andrews*, vol. 2, pp. 381–388.

than in theology ''. He was chaplain to the Earl of Rothes, and was formerly minister of North Leith and Duns.[1]

James Hamilton was admitted into Holy Orders by the Archbishop of Glasgow in 1634, and was inducted minister of Cambusnethan, where he continued till the Restoration.[2]

Robert Leighton was educated at Edinburgh University and later, for about ten years, travelled in England and on the Continent. Dr. Archibald Main writes: '' Robert Leighton was not representative of his age or his fellows—indeed, he was neither a persistent Presbyterian nor a typical Episcopalian, and if he was uncomfortable with many of his Covenanting brethren, he was equally unhappy with some of his prelatic friends. In him, piety and Erastianism made a strange mixture. Certainly he had in him the making of a martyr, and he preferred the role of the obedient citizen before that of the saint. But the Archbishop[3] was a saint. No one can appreciate him who fails to discover his real saintliness of life. He failed in his ecclesiastical statesmanship, he was not a good judge of men and affairs, he lacked the qualities of leadership and inspiration; but mysterious as is the story of his life, he achieved much by the genuine goodness of his soul.'' Leighton was inducted to the parish of Newbattle in 1640, and there his active ministry really began. Twelve years later he was appointed Principal of the University of Edinburgh.[4]

The Consecrations

James Sharp, Andrew Fairfoull, James Hamilton, and Robert Leighton were solemnly consecrated Bishops in Westminster

---

[1] Keith, *Catalogue*, p. 265.   [2] Ib., p. 281.
[3] Leighton became Archbishop of Glasgow in 1672.
[4] Pearson, *Life of Archbishop Leighton*; Burnet, *History of His Own Time*, vol. 1, pp. 228–239; Butler, *Life and Letters of Robert Leighton*; E. Knox, *Robert Leighton, a study of his life, times and writings*. The quotation in the text is from the Foreword to Bishop Knox's volume, written by Dr. Main, formerly Professor of Ecclesiastical History at Glasgow University. Kirkton, with his strong prejudice against Episcopacy, which seems to blind his eyes to the truth and distorts the facts, describes Bishop Leighton as '' almost destitute of a doctrinal principle ''.

Abbey in December 1661 by the Bishops of London, Worcester, Carlisle, and Llandaff. Sharp and Leighton were ordained deacons and priests before their consecration to the Episcopate.

In the same month the Scottish Privy Council issued a proclamation, which was published at the market cross of every town. It enjoined that in future patrons of parishes must present their nominees to the Bishop, who would induct and admit. Further, it strictly prohibited the Presbyterians from exercising the functions of induction and admission.

On their return to Scotland the new Bishops officiated at their first Consecration Service in Holyrood on May 7th, 1662. The consecrators, Archbishops Sharp and Fairfoull and Bishop Hamilton, were " clothed in their white surplices under their black gowns, except their sleeves, which were all of them white, of delicate cambric and lawn ". The seven Bishops consecrated were George Haliburton for Dunkeld, David Strachan for Brechin, John Paterson for Ross, Murdock MacKenzie for Moray, Patrick Forbes for Caithness, Robert Wallace for the Isles, and David Fletcher for ·Argyll. Later, David Mitchell and George Wishart were consecrated Bishops for Aberdeen and Edinburgh respectively.[1]

The Church was now possessed of its full number of Bishops, and churchpeople extended their welcome to them as they took up their places in the ancient dioceses.

Election of Bishops

As dioceses fell vacant in the natural course of events, the following method was observed for the election of Bishops. The Chapter of the vacant see elected the person recommended by the King, whose patent under the Great Seal confirmed the election of the Chapter, by which the right of the Bishop-elect to the spiritualities of the see was legalized. A royal mandate

[1] Grub, vol. 3, pp. 187–199.

was then issued for the consecration, at which three Bishops at least were to be present. The Bishop, however, could not administer the temporalities of his see until he did homage and swore obedience to the sovereign.

Bishops and Parliament

The first Act passed in the Parliament which met in May 1662 was for " calling the Bishops to the Parliament ". The Act recalled that the Clergy once represented the first Estate in the constitution of Parliament; now that Archbishops and Bishops are restored, " it is fit the Parliament be returned to its ancient constitution, and the Clergy have their place and vote as formerly ".[1]

The Administration of the Church

In the early years of the Restoration period several Acts of Parliament were passed which bear on Church administration. One of the problems was to deal with those ministers who possessed benefices and stipends without presentation from the lawful patrons. King Charles II, acting on the advice of Parliament, ordered that all such ministers who entered into their parishes in or since the year 1649 had no right to their places or stipends and that as from 1662 " their places, benefices and kirks are *ipso jure* vacant ". At the same time His Majesty called upon every such minister to obtain a presentation from the lawful patron and have collation from the Bishop of the diocese and thus have the right to enjoy his church benefice. The patrons were further enjoined to grant presentations to all the then incumbents, or to provide a substitute for those who refused, by March 1663, after which the presentations were to lapse to the Bishop of the diocese according to the former laws.

A number of Acts were passed in 1662 regulating the teinds

---

[1] *Acts P.S.*, vol. 7, pp. 367–406.

belonging to Bishops and other beneficed persons, ordering that all persons in public trust renounce by a signed declaration the National Covenant and the Solemn League and Covenant, and announcing the King's gracious and free pardon, act of indemnity, and oblivion, to all except such persons as had forfeited their rights or been declared fugitives in the present Parliament or by the Committee of Estates since August 1660.[1]

Later in the same year the Privy Council issued an " Act for holding of Diocesan Assemblies " which set forth that as the Bishops were returning to their dioceses after the Parliamentary Session to hold their Diocesan Assemblies, all incumbents were enjoined to resort to these Assemblies on pain of being treated as " contemners of His Majesty's authority, incurring the censures provided in such cases ". This Act also declared that all who held any other ecclesiastical meetings were to be " holden henceforth as seditious ". All meetings of Synods, Presbyteries, and Kirk Sessions had been prohibited, unless by the appointment of the Archbishops and Bishops.

A meeting of the Privy Council at Glasgow published an Act discharging all incumbents who had no lawful presentations from the patrons and who would not receive collation from the Bishops. As a result some two hundred preachers in the Western Counties were discharged, and general discontentment was stirred up amongst the Covenanters. The vast majority of the incumbents in Scotland conformed. Dr. McCrie declared that out of 600 Resolutioners, 560 conformed without much reluctance. In the counties of Perth, Stirling, and Fife and in the counties north of the Tay there was a general willingness to accept the collation of the Bishops. In the south of Scotland, however, and chiefly in the south-west, many preachers were deprived.

There does not appear to have been any uniform practice by the Restoration Bishops with regard to the ordination of Presbyterian preachers or ministers. Bishops Wishart in Edinburgh

---

[1] *Acts P.S.*, vol. 7, pp. 367–406.

and Mitchell in Aberdeen were probably stricter than most of the others, for it appears that several of the Bishops ruled with such moderation and forbearance that they were unwilling to do more than persuade presbyterian preachers to accept ordination. The law did not concern itself with ordination, as such, but with episcopal jurisdiction, and the rights of the Bishops to grant collation to those nominated by the lawful patrons. W. R. Foster, in his study *Bishop and Presbytery*, states " The practice of ordination by the Bishop was quite universal according to all the extant records available, and none of the exceptions which were permissible in the licensing of preachers occurred when ordination was in question. Those who sought ordination came to the Bishop, and the service usually took place in his church."[1]

Several Bishops, and notably Archbishop Sharp, appointed Kirk Sessions and Presbyteries as well as Diocesan Synods. Parliament passed an Act in 1663 " for the establishment and constitution of a National Synod ". The members of the Synod were to be the two Archbishops and their suffragan Bishops, Deans of Cathedral Churches and Archdeacons, and certain Moderators and other presbyters, with representatives from the Universities. The Synod was to meet on the King's appointment, and was to consider matters relating to doctrine, worship, discipline, and the government of the Church, and its president was to be the Archbishop of St. Andrews. No act of the Synod was to be valid which was contrary to the royal prerogative or the laws of the kingdom, or which was not approved by His Majesty or his commissioners.[2]

Divine Worship

No Liturgy was introduced, but the Westminster Directory for public worship was set aside. The clergy were enjoined to

---

[1] W. R. Foster, *Bishop and Presbytery*, p. 96 (*see also* Gordon Donaldson, *Scottish Historical Review*, 1954, p. 172).   [2] *Acts P.S.*, vol. 7, p. 465.

use the Lord's Prayer and the Doxology, and parents and others who presented children for Baptism were to declare their belief in the Christian Faith as defined in the Apostles' Creed. Holy Communion was administered in the Presbyterian way with the people sitting at long tables; there were no organs in the churches, and the distinctive dress of the clergy was the black gown. Some of the Bishops, and notably Bishop Leighton, enjoined the clergy of their dioceses to discourage the people from " their most indecent practice of sitting in time of prayer ", and to persuade them either to stand or kneel, so that both with bodies and with souls they might worship Him who made both soul and body for that end. Injunctions were also given to warn the people against neglect in attending at the celebration of the Holy Communion. The ordination of presbyters and the consecration of Bishops generally followed the forms of the Church of England. Archbishop Alexander Burnet of Glasgow is described by Gilbert Burnet in his *Memorial of Grievances* as " a mighty bigot for the English ceremonies and forms, and as forward to have all the usages of that church introduced to Scotland, as if he had been educated by Bishop Laud. At his first diocesan meeting, he put five or six curates publicly in orders after the English pontifical to inure the West of Scotland to these novelties." There was also a Scottish rite of ordination in use, as for example by Bishop MacKenzie. Bishops ordained ministers after their examination by the Presbytery. Ordination by the Presbytery alone ceased. In the consecration of Bishops the practice of three consecrators was maintained.

The services in the established Episcopal Church of the Restoration must have been as bare as in some of the smaller Presbyterian sects of the present time, and such as few modern Presbyterians would tolerate. A reformer of the Aberdeen diocese, James Gordon of Banchory-Devenick, suggested in *The Reformed Bishop* that there be a gradual restoration of liturgical worship by ecclesiastical authority. His work was published in 1679.[1]

The Insurrection of the Covenanters

Previously in the Restoration period the laws against Non-conformity had been strictly observed, though without bloodshed, but in 1666 open insurrection flared up on the part of Covenanters in the west, who issued a manifesto complaining of the oppression to which they were subjected and declaring the necessity of taking up arms on behalf of their principles. This revolt was punished with great severity, and many of those who took part were executed.[2]

Several attempts were made to conciliate deprived ministers, and to restore tranquillity to the Church. A general plan of comprehension by which Presbyterians might be persuaded to conform found a ready champion in Robert Leighton. His scheme for a constitutional Episcopacy provided a place for the ecclesiastical courts of Presbyterianism. The Bishops were to preside in their Synods, but to be guided by the majority of their presbyters.

The King, in a letter to the Privy Council, 1669, declared that any of the ejected ministers who had acted in an orderly and quiet manner might be reinstated in their former charges, if vacant, or presented to other charges, provided that they accepted collation from the Bishop. Failing this, an indulgence was offered giving permission to officiate in a parish, and offering a small stipend with the right to occupy the manse. Forty ministers accepted the indulgence. This measure was most unpopular. It set aside the canonical authority of the Episcopate, while it laid the " indulged ministers " under the charge of submitting to the King. They were popularly described as

---

[1] He advocated the free election of Bishops as well as a gradual restoration of liturgical worship. He was censured by the Bishops chiefly because of his criticism of them as men out of sympathy with the teaching and traditions of the Church. [2] Burnet, *History*, vol. 1, pp. 404–414.

" the King's curates ". The Archbishop of Glasgow, Burnet, and the clergy in Synod protested against the indulgence and the King's interference.

Meanwhile, rebellious voices found opportunity to incite the malcontents in the south-west at open-air conventicles. The danger to public peace was real.

Therefore, in 1670, Parliament passed an Act against Conventicles, by which all persons, except the established clergy and the indulged ministers, were forbidden to preach, expound the scripture, or pray, at any meeting, unless in their own houses or families, under pain of imprisonment. Any who attended such meetings were declared liable to heavy fines. Further, because open meetings in the fields tended to the encouragement of rebellion, any who preached at or conducted such meetings were made liable to the penalty of death and the confiscation of their goods, and those who attended made liable to fines.[1]

In 1672 an indulgence was granted to certain ministers who had been ejected since 1661, allowing them to preach in certain parishes and to receive a portion of the benefice income for their support.[2] This partial toleration seemed to encourage the Nonconformists, and attendance at field-meetings became a sort of passion, the danger apparently making it more attractive. At any rate, the Covenanters became bolder in their opposition to the Church, and field-preaching became more and more common. When the Government attempted to put down these meetings by force, the people did not scruple to offer resistance. Covenanting criticism of the Episcopate seemed to be centred on the Primate, Archbishop Sharp, who was waylaid near St. Andrews, by a party of fanatics, as an enemy of the Gospel, " a murderer of the saints, and a betrayer of the Church ", and cruelly murdered.[3]

[1] Acts P.S., vol. 8, pp. 9–10, 71, 89; Burnet, History, vol. 1, pp. 505–507, 586–591.

[2] Wodrow, History, vol. 2, pp. 203–210; Burnet, History, vol. 1, pp. 591–592.

[3] Wodrow, History, vol. 3, pp. 41–51; Burnet, History, vol. 2, pp. 226–227.

The fanaticism of the Nonconformists and the cruelty of the Government removed any hope of peace or even the possibility of reaching an accommodation. Parliament passed a Test Act in 1681 by which all persons holding any office in Church or State were obliged to swear that they professed the true Protestant Religion as contained in the Confession of Faith ratified by the first Parliament of James the Sixth; that they acknowledged the King's Majesty as the only supreme governor of the realm; that it was unlawful for subjects to enter into covenants or leagues, or to assemble in council or convention to treat of matters affecting the Church or State, without his permission; that it was unlawful to take up arms against him; that there lay no obligation upon them from the National Covenant or the Solemn League and Covenant, or in any other way, to try to change the government of Church and State then established by law; and that they would never decline His Majesty's power and jurisdiction. [1]

There was widespread criticism of the Test Act, even on the part of churchmen. Some of the clergy in the diocese of Aberdeen objected to receiving the Confession of Faith as the standard of their belief because some passages in it were obscure and doubtful and some contrary to the doctrine of their own and other reformed Churches. After discussion had taken place in the Diocesan Synods, an explanation of the Test was published by which the prelates were authorized to administer the oaths to the clergy in the sense that they did not swear to every proposition or clause in the Confession of Faith but only to the true Protestant religion, founded in the Word of God, contained in that Confession, as it was opposed to Popery and fanaticism; that by the Test no encroachment was made on the intrinsic spiritual power of the Church; and that the oath and Test were without any prejudice to the Episcopal government of the Church. This explanation received the royal sanction and was accepted by most

[1] *Acts P.S.*, vol. 8, pp. 243–244.

of the clergy. About eighty clergy, however, were not satisfied with the explanation and resigned their charges, generally accepting benefices in England.[1] Amongst those who opposed the Test was the Earl of Argyll, who was impeached and condemned for refusing to accept it. Fearing the worst from the tyranny of the Court of Justiciary, Argyll made his escape from Edinburgh to Holland. The Court passed sentence of death upon him in his absence, and under this uncancelled sentence he was executed early in the reign of James VII.

At this point in our narrative it is convenient to consider the conduct of the Covenanters, who were chiefly centred in south-west Scotland. Their banner bore the significant words, " No Quarter for the Active Enemies of the Covenant." Andrew Lang writes: " The Covenanters are popularly supposed to have been martyrs for freedom of conscience. The very reverse is the fact; or rather, they were martyrs for a conscience which urged them to persecute the consciences of others." After a skirmish at Drumclog, in which thirty-six Government troopers were killed, as against three Covenanters, Hamilton, the leader of the Covenanters, who had put to death with his own hands one of the prisoners, was furious that five others had escaped, contrary to his orders that no quarter should be given to " Babel's brats ".

News of the Drumclog " victory " spread like wildfire, and a little later the Covenanters prepared for battle at Bothwell Bridge. On this occasion, however, they suffered a severe defeat; four hundred fell in the fight, and twelve hundred were made prisoners and taken to Edinburgh. Two ministers, leaders of the rebellion, were executed at the Grassmarket, and five others were hanged on Magus Moor in silly revenge for the murder of Archbishop Sharp. The other prisoners were penned together for some months in Greyfriars Churchyard. Some were freed on promising not to take up arms again against the King,

[1] Burnet, *History*, vol. 2, pp. 301–314.

but about two hundred and fifty were shipped for Barbados; the vessel was wrecked, however, on one of the Orkney islands, and most of them were drowned.

Richard Cameron and his followers, who became known as the Cameronians, continued the struggle. Various indulgences were offered by the Government, but the Covenanters did not wish anything less than the complete victory of their cause and the power to enforce their will. The Cameronians now declared themselves openly opposed to monarchy as leading to tyranny. In the declaration at Sanquhar, they stated: '' We disown Charles Stewart that has been reigning, or rather tyrannising on the throne of Britain these years bygone. We being under the standard of our Lord Jesus Christ, Captain of Salvation, do declare a war with such tyrant and usurper.'' [1]

In this sorely troubled era there were several voices calling for peace. Chief amongst them was Bishop Leighton, who was prepared to commend a compromise which, while preserving characteristic features of Presbyterian discipline, also preserved a constitutional Episcopacy. He constantly preached peace and inspired his representatives in the south-west, the Bishop's Evangelists as they were called, to call for peace. He declared, ''My sole object has been to procure peace, and to advance the interests of true religion.'' At first as Commendator and later as Archbishop of Glasgow, Leighton urged his pacific policy, but in the end, in 1674, he returned to England, deeply disappointed in the failure of his efforts.

Accession of James VII

On the death of Charles II in 1685, James VII, who as Duke of York had acquired a reputation as a persecutor of the Covenanters, was proclaimed King. The Cameronians lost no time in declaring their intention of punishing, according to their power, as enemies of God and the covenanted work of the Refor-

[1] Wodrow, *History*, vol. 4, pp. 148–165.

mation, all who should assist in putting the existing laws into execution. Soon afterwards they murdered two gentlemen of the King's life-guard. Parliament replied in an Act which declared that the giving, taking, or owning of the National Covenant or the Solemn League and Covenant was treason; and further, that all persons who took part in field-conventicles were to be punished with death or confiscation of goods.

A Policy of General Toleration

By a Royal Proclamation in 1687, the King gave permission to the moderate Presbyterians to meet at their private houses and hear all such ministers as were willing to accept this indulgence; to the Quakers to meet in any place appointed for their worship; and to Roman Catholics to celebrate their religious services in houses or chapels. The King also declared that he would employ indifferently all his subjects, of whatever persuasion, so that none should meet with discouragement on account of their religion.

Later, another Proclamation suspended all penal laws against Nonconformity, and all the King's subjects were allowed to meet and serve God in their own way, either in private houses, or chapels, or places built or hired for the purpose, on condition that nothing disloyal should be taught on those occasions, that the places of meeting should be open to all, and that the names of the places and the preachers should be made known to the Government. The Presbyterians generally welcomed the policy of general toleration, and an address of thanks to His Majesty was drawn up by Nonconformist ministers in Edinburgh.[1]

This toleration, however, did not extend to field-conventicles, and the Cameronians continued to give trouble. One of their leaders, James Renwick, was apprehended early in 1688 and, condemned by the Court of Justiciary, he was executed.

---

[1] Wodrow, ib., pp. 416–437; Burnet, *History*, vol. 3, pp. 171–173, *Vindication of Church and State in Scotland*, pp. 148–154.

He was the last to suffer death in the cause of the Covenant. [1]

It is clear that the policy of toleration pursued by James was partly because of his desire to favour Romanists. He ordered that the abbey church of Holyrood be fitted for Roman Catholic worship, and he allowed the Jesuits to take possession of the church and to set up a printing-press. His determination to favour his co-religionists brought opposition from several of the Bishops. Bishop Bruce of Dunkeld and Archbishop Cairncross of Glasgow were deprived because of their opposition.

It is reasonable to suppose that the country would have settled down in due course had not the attempt of James VII to restore Romanism renewed fears which had been lingering in the minds of many Scotspeople ever since the beginning of the reign of Charles II. The trial of the Seven Bishops in England led to the Revolution of 1688. William, Prince of Orange, was invited by representatives of the English Parliament to lead the opposition and, already, before rebellion could be organized, James escaped from England. The Whig party in London offered the crown to William and Mary, though most of the Seven English Bishops who had been imprisoned in the Tower of London were unwilling to break their oath of allegiance to James, and were consequently deprived of their sees. All the Scottish Bishops and most of the other clergy felt bound by their allegiance to James, and so William gave his support to the Presbyterians.

Canon J. A. MacCulloch, D.D., a scholarly priest of the Church in Scotland, published in successive issues of the *Scottish Guardian* (February–April, 1949) a valuable paper on the Episcopal Church of the Restoration period. In this paper he deals with the charge that the clergy of the Restoration were very young, very ignorant, very incompetent, and scandalous in their lives, and alleges that this was the slander put out by their reckless opponents. He writes, " It is mainly, though not solely, found in the book by James Kirkton, *The Secret and True History of the Church of Scotland*, and is maintained in current belief and also by historians who have not investigated matters for themselves." Apart from a small area in the south-west, the majority of the congregations in Scotland were tired of the Covenants and were satisfied with their ministers' having conformed to Episcopacy. Many of these ministers retained their livings long after the Revolution of 1689— their people had no sympathy with the fanatical Covenanters of the south-west.

[1] Carslaw, *Life of James Renwick*, pp. 1–37, 147–176.

The view that all Scotland was Covenanting, and consequently persecuted, is described as a " grotesque and unfair picture of Scottish history and religious life " in the Restoration period. " The Covenanters were in a minority in Scotland, a minority unyielding and implacable in its hatred of the new order." " The Covenanting leaders were one and all rebels and anarchists, who intended to leave no stone unturned, if only they could force with violence everyone to their own way of thinking, or failing that to put them to death."

Dr. MacCulloch carefully describes in this paper the distorted view of history presented by Kirkton and Wodrow, and glibly repeated by others, and then writes, " The seven volumes of the *Fasti Ecclesiae Scoticanae*, with its sober statement of facts about the ministers and clergy from the Reformation onwards, offers a contrast between the slanderous tradition and the actual truth." The contrast throws a vivid light on the malicious nonsense written about the Episcopal Church and its clergy from 1660 to 1689 and later. The total number of parishes in Scotland at the Restoration was over 900, of which 96 were vacant. Out of these some 274 ministers were deprived, of which 135 were in the Synods of Glasgow, Ayr, Dumfries, and Galloway. However, about 120 of the deprived ministers returned to their parishes under the Indulgences of 1669 and 1672. It is clear therefore that the great majority of the clergy before the Restoration continued to minister during the Restoration period.

Of the clergy ordained during the period, if we confine our attention to the south-west (Glasgow, Ayr, Dumfries, and Galloway), eighty-one were ordained to fill vacant charges in 1662 and soon after, and of these thirty were graduates of Edinburgh, twenty-five were graduates of Glasgow, nine were graduates of St. Andrews, and fifteen were graduates of Aberdeen. After selecting numerous statistics and considering them, Dr. MacCulloch adds, " These tedious details have been given to show that Kirkton, in alleging that the ' curats ' were youthful, ignorant, and ' wholly fetched out of the north country ', was malicious and incorrect, and that those who follow his leading, or rather misleading, are in error. Those clergy ordained in 1662 or succeeding years were no younger than Presbyterian ministers of the period when ordained, and most of them were not very young. Graduates of a University (even of Aberdeen!) are not usually ' unstudied and unbred '."

Dealing with the charge of scandalous living, Canon MacCulloch first remarks that the statements of Kirkton and Wodrow are suspect because of their proved unrelenting prejudice against Episcopalians. (Thus Kirkton says of the clergy, " The body of them were so debauched a company, common people would not believe an honest man would continue in their company.") After presenting a careful summary of the charges preferred against clergy during the Restoration period, he states, " While it is sad that even this comparatively small number of deprivals for drunkenness or immorality should have occurred, they are spread over a period of 29 years, and by no means correspond to the general accusations of the Presbyterian historians, like those of Kirkton and Wodrow." " The actual deprivations show that the Bishops were careful to see that the lives of their clergy were such as they should be."

" The ' ignorant ' clergy of the Restoration period who survived the year of the Revolution were not deficient in authorship. Most of their writings, and they were many, were of a theological kind."

3

THE DISESTABLISHMENT OF THE CHURCH

The Action of the Bishops

THE immediate cause of the disestablishment was the action of the Bishops themselves. They refused to accept the mutual support offered by William. Soon after he had arrived in England he summoned Dr. Alexander Rose, Bishop of Edinburgh, to an interview at Whitehall. Bishop Rose was in London as commissary and representative of his brethren at this crisis. In the course of the interview, William expressed a hope that the Scottish Bishops would be kind to him and follow the example of England. To this, the Bishop replied, " Sir, I will serve you so far as law, reason, or conscience shall allow me ". The Prince broke off the conversation and turned away. In recording this occurrence in a letter to Bishop Campbell in 1713, Dr. Rose shows that there was no doubt about the meaning of the Prince's words and the Bishop's answer.[1] There is good reason to suppose that Episcopacy in Scotland would have retained its hold to this day if William had received the answer he seemed to expect. For though William had Presbyterian predilections, he was much more concerned about his political interests, and was not likely to make any such implied overture to Bishop Rose and his brethren unless he felt assured that his cause would be at least as safe in their hands as in those of the Presbyterian leaders, who were only too ready to welcome and espouse it.

It has been customary with Episcopalian writers to speak of the Bishops as noble champions of a chivalrous loyalty, as devoted

[1] See Appendix A.

26

witnesses to the truth, and as sufferers for conscience' sake. The other side of the picture might reveal sentiments of narrow nationalism, as, for example, irritation at the dethronement of a Scottish King in favour of a foreigner by an English Parliament, perhaps also a sense of obligation to the Stuarts, who had befriended Episcopacy in the past, with the suspicion that they alone could be relied upon to defend it in days to come, and perhaps also a deep-seated feeling of jealousy towards England.

" Rabbling " of Episcopal Clergy

The south-west of Scotland became the scene of lawless disorder after the flight of James VII. On the withdrawal of the military into England, the Cameronian peasantry armed themselves and in committees perambulated the country to evict and maltreat the Episcopal clergy, or, as the phrase has it, to " rabble the curates ". More than a hundred such clergy were violently ejected from their churches and manses during the winter of 1688–1689.[1]

Bishop Rose, in London, sought support and help on behalf of the suffering clergy of the north. Bishop Compton of London advised an approach to William on the subject of the persecution and at the same time to congratulate him on the success of his expedition. As a loyal Jacobite, Bishop Rose could not do this. Dean Scott of Glasgow followed Bishop Rose to London with a petition from the Archbishop of Glasgow and the western clergy craving protection from persecution. William replied by ordering a proclamation to be made forbidding all disturbance and violence.

The Establishment of Presbyterianism

In March 1689 the Convention of Estates, numbering one hundred and fifty members from the Three Estates, including the two Archbishops and seven Bishops, met in Edinburgh. The

[1] Burnet, *History*, vol. 3, p. 344.

elected President, the Duke of Hamilton, endeavoured to persuade the Primate and the Bishop of Edinburgh to cast in their lot with William for the sake of the Church, assuring them that he had the Prince's word that nothing would be done to the prejudice of Episcopacy if the Bishops would support him.

Letters were read in the Convention both from King James and from William. James offered a free pardon to all who should return to their allegiance within a month, and denounced as traitors those who should not. William expressed his desire that the Convention should settle the religion and liberties of the nation upon a broad and liberal basis. Several of the royalists left the Convention, and the remaining members proceeded with the business. It was declared that James had forfeited his right to the crown and that the throne was vacant. The crown was then offered to William and Mary, and all ministers were enjoined to make proclamations accordingly in church and to pray for the new sovereign under pain of deprivation. The resolutions were embodied in the Claim of Right, one of the statements of which is: " Prelacy and the superiority of any office in the Church above Presbyters is, and hath been, a great and insupportable grievance and trouble to this nation, and contrary to the inclination of the people, ever since the Reformation (they having been reformed from Popery by Presbyters) and therefore ought to be abolished." [1]

William and Mary accepted the crown, but in accepting the Coronation oath William made it clear that he would not be a persecutor. Many Episcopal clergy were deposed at this time as Non-Jurors.

In July 1689 an Act was introduced before the Estates whereby prelacy and all superiority of office in the Church above presbyters were to be abolished and the King and Queen were to settle the government of the Church in the way most agreeable to the inclinations of the people. While the draft of the Act was

[1] *Acts P.S.*, vol. 9, pp. 98, 104–106, 117–134, 163, 196, 199.

being considered, an address was received from the commissioners of the Diocesan Synod of Aberdeen earnestly supplicating the Estates to convene a free General Assembly for the rectifying of disorders, the healing of divisions, and the settlement of the polity of the Church.[1] The Presbyterians opposed with energy the calling of an Assembly, because the Episcopal clergy would have outnumbered and outvoted the Presbyterians by six to one.

And so Episcopacy was disestablished by the Scottish Parliament in July 1689 without the voice of the General Assembly having been heard. In April of the following year the Act of 1669 was repealed, and those Presbyterian ministers who had been deprived since 1661 for Nonconformity were restored and their Episcopal successors were ordered to remove from the churches, manses, and glebes before Whitsunday ensuing. Three months later, in June 1690, the Three Estates of peers, barons, and burgesses ratified the Westminster Confession of Faith and established the Presbyterian form of government and discipline.

The Disestablished Church

Many differing estimates are quoted of the relative number of Episcopalians and Presbyterians at the time of the Revolution, but there is ample evidence in support of the contention that " more than two-thirds of the people of the country, and most part of the gentry, were Episcopals ", in the words of Dr. Carlyle of Inveresk in his autobiography.[2]

Writing to a friend at the end of 1690, a zealous Presbyterian, General MacKay, said, " I tell you who know Scotland, and where the strength and weakness of it doth lie, that if I were as much an enemy to that interest [the Presbyterian] as I am a friend, I would without difficulty engage to form in Scotland a more formidable party against it, even for their majesties' govern-

[1] A copy of the Aberdeen address is preserved amongst the Papers of the Episcopal Church in Scotland (see p. 163, n.).
[2] Grub, vol. 3, pp. 315–318.

ment, than can be formed for it." [1]   Writing in the same year, an Episcopalian, Lord Tarbet, said, " The Presbyterians are the more zealous and hotter; the other more numerous and powerful."

In the early years of its disestablished life the Church had no capable leader. Indeed its policy appears to have been one of aimless drift, remarkable only for an ardent devotion to the fallen line of Stuarts. Almost at once the Church passed under a cloud, and the Bishops continued their ministrations " with mournful privacy ". Many of the clergy would have agreed for the sake of peace to acknowledge William. Some were ready to accept a Presbyterian form of government, and William was not unwilling to accept them in the new Establishment, but the Presbyterian ministers opposed any attempts to accommodate them. The majority of the clergy, however, followed the Bishops and remained loyal Jacobites.

Ejection of University Professors

The Scottish nobility and gentry who remained loyal to the Episcopal Church were soon joined by senators of the College of Justice and Professors of the Universities. A Special Act of Parliament in 1690 required the Principals, Professors, Regents, and Masters of the Universities to subscribe the Westminster Confession, take the oaths of allegiance, and submit to Presbyterian government. Most of the Principals and Professors refused to do so and were ejected from their offices and thrown penniless upon the world. [2]

The State of the Church

We have already noted that the disestablished Church was numerically strong, especially north of the Tay, that the greater

[1] General MacKay's letter is preserved in the General Register House, Edinburgh.

[2] Lawson, *History of the Scottish Episcopal Church*, pp. 109–110; cf. Grub, vol. 3, pp. 315–318.

part of the nobility and the gentry, with most of the Professors of the Universities, were Episcopalians and that many were ready to suffer for their loyalty. In spite of repeated attempts to eject them, many of the clergy, particularly in the northern charges, were able to continue their ministrations in the parish churches because of the vigorous loyalty of their congregations. Many others gathered their congregations in meeting-houses, as for example when Bishop Rose led his people from St. Giles Cathedral, Edinburgh, to a former wool-store as their first meeting-place.

Though the Church was disestablished and disendowed, yet there is reason to believe that, freed from state control and state interference, it might have gone forward to develop its worship and witness and to build up its resources if it had had good and capable leaders amongst its Bishops and if it had not been tied to the fortunes of the Stuart line of kings.

Archbishop Ross of St. Andrews occupied the position of leadership as Primate of the Church, but he lacked the qualities of a great leader. Archbishop Paterson of Glasgow was a violent supporter of the fallen dynasty. Bishop Rose of Edinburgh, who outlived all his contemporaries, felt like others of his brethren that he could not conscientiously break the allegiance he had sworn to James VII and that it was only necessary to wait patiently for the return of his acknowledged King, when the Church would once again be restored.[1]

Given good leadership the Church might soon have weathered the difficulties which were already troubling it, but the Bishops failed to give the guidance necessary, and the history of the next few decades appears to suggest that the Church drifted aimlessly from year to year without a plan or policy.

[1] Keith, *Catalogue*.

4

PERSECUTION AND TOLERATION

A General Assembly

THE King appointed a General Assembly to be held at Edinburgh in October 1690. About one hundred and eighty ministers and elders attended, but none of them came from beyond the Tay, and only one represented the Universities. The King's Letter advised moderation, stating, " We never could be of the mind that violence was suited to the advancing of true religion. Moderation is what religion enjoins, neighbouring churches expect from, and we recommend to you."

An Act of the Assembly required all ministers, probationers, and elders to subscribe the Westminster Confession. Private Communion of the sick and House Baptisms were forbidden. Two Commissions of Visitation were appointed to supervise the restoration of order and with particular reference to the Episcopal clergy who still held parishes. A day of fasting was appointed for the sins of the nation, including that of the recent establishment of prelacy and the decay of true godliness resulting from it.[1]

Another Assembly

Two years later, when another General Assembly met, most of the members came from south of the Tay. Dr. Cunningham gives as the reason why no Presbyterians came from the north " simply that there were no Presbyterians to come ".[2] A letter was read from the King in which he said, " It has been represented

[1] *Acts G.A.*, pp. 221–235; *Historical Relation of the General Assembly of 1690*, pp. 16–64; Skinner, *Ecclesiastical History of Scotland*, vol. 2, pp. 567–575.

[2] Cunningham, *History of the Church of Scotland*, vol. 2, p. 298.

to us that you are not a full Assembly, there being as great a number of ministers of the Church of Scotland as you are who are not allowed to be represented." He enjoined that the Episcopal clergy should be admitted upon signing a formula and declaration and that the two Commissions for settling ministers should be composed equally of Presbyterians and Episcopalians. The Assembly refused to admit conforming Episcopal clergy, and was dissolved by the King's command.[1]

The Problem of Filling Vacant Charges

The Presbyterian Establishment found many difficulties in the matter of filling vacant charges. Many of the southern clergy had already been ejected by " rabbling ", and some of these had gone to England and Ireland, a few of whom later found places in the American colonies. In the north, however, the situation was altogether different, since the Episcopalian clergy continued to occupy their churches and manses for several years. Nevertheless, in spite of the acute shortage of " qualified " ministers and the fact that the majority of the churches in the south were vacant, every opportunity was taken, and often with the help of the military, to depose the Episcopalian clergy of the north.

In Stewart's *Sketches of the Highlands*, an interesting account is given of an attempt to intrude a Presbyterian minister into the parish of Glenorchy: "The late Episcopal clergyman of the parish of Glenorchy, Mr. David Lindsay, was ordered to surrender his charge to a Presbyterian minister then appointed by the Earl of Argyll. When the new minister reached his parish to take possession of his living, not an individual would speak to him, except Mr. Lindsay himself, who received him kindly. On Sunday the new clergyman went to church accompanied by his

[1] Grub, vol. 3, pp. 328–330; Cunningham, vol. 2, p. 300. Cunningham writes, "Notwithstanding all the ejections which had taken place the Episcopalians still formed a majority in the church, and if they were admitted to a vote in the Church's judicatories they might form and fashion matters as they pleased."

predecessor. The whole population of the district were assembled, but they would not enter the church. No person spoke to the new minister, nor was there the least noise or violence till he attempted to enter the church, when he was surrounded by twelve men fully armed, who told him he must accompany them; and disregarding all Mr. Lindsay's prayers and entreaties, they ordered the piper to play the march of death, and marched away the minister to the confines of the parish. Here they made him swear on the Bible that he would never return or attempt to disturb Mr. Lindsay. He kept his oath, and Mr. Lindsay lived thirty years afterwards, and died Episcopal minister of Glenorchy, loved and revered by his flock." [1]

Persecution and Torture

Large numbers of the Jacobite nobility and gentry, and many others, were imprisoned, and some of them were tortured, in the Edinburgh Tolbooth, Stirling Castle, Blackness Castle, the Bass Rock, and other places of confinement. [2]

The Scottish Parliament which met in April 1693 passed the Oath of Assurance calling on all persons holding civil or ecclesiastical office, whether Presbyterian or Episcopalian, to swear that William was King both *de jure* and *de facto*. Many Episcopalians who had accepted the simpler oath of allegiance were unable to admit the King's legal title. Later in the same year, an Act was passed " for settling the peace and quiet of the church ". It declared that no person should be a minister of the Established Church unless he had taken the oath of allegiance and that of assurance, subscribed the Westminster Confession, and accepted the Presbyterian government as the only government of the Church. [3] The General Assembly readily endorsed the second Act and proceeded to enforce it upon Episcopal clergy still in legal possession of their parishes. As late as eighteen years

---

[1] Stewart, *Sketches of the Highlands*, vol. 1, p. 99; Lawson, pp. 128–145.
[2] Chambers, *Domestic Annals of Scotland*, vol. 3, pp. 10–15, 60–68, and also, for the siege of Bass Rock, pp. 95–97.   [3] *Acts P.S.*, vol. 9, pp. 262–264.

after the Revolution there were a hundred and sixty-five Episcopal incumbents ministering in parishes where local feeling was too strong to permit of their ejection. A Commission was sent to Aberdeen in 1694 to enforce the statute, and was met by a Committee appointed to represent a large number of the clergy of the seven northern dioceses. The Committee presented two documents, the first containing a series of questions challenging the right of fifty or sixty Presbyterian ministers to speak in the name of the Church of Scotland, and the second a protest against recent Assemblies, which, they declared, did not represent the National Church.[1]

A further Act was passed by the Scottish Parliament in 1695 which forbade the deprived Episcopal clergy to celebrate Baptisms or Marriages under pain of imprisonment.[2] (Later, Parliament offered an indulgence to clergy who had not taken the oaths, by extending the time for qualifying. More than a hundred clergy accepted the indulgence offered.) Nevertheless, unseemly rioting continued to take place when the new claimants sought to take possession of their livings, and generally churches and churchyards were the scenes of the riots. Laypeople continued to demonstrate their determination to prevent the Presbyterian minister from entering the church, in spite of the support of the law. This kind of rioting spread from parish to parish, and in 1698 Parliament passed an Act " for preventing of disorders in the supplying and planting of vacant churches ".[3]

Thus by various devices, through Acts of Parliament or through the activities of General Assembly Commissions, with the combined forces of the military and the Presbyteries, efforts were continually being made to destroy the support the Church possessed

---

[1] Spalding Club, *Miscellany*, vol. 2, pp. 163–171. In the diocese of Aberdeen, out of about one hundred parishes, there was one Presbyterian minister in 1690; there were eight in 1694 and fifteen in 1697.

[2] *Acts P.S.*, vol. 9, pp. 387, 449–450.

[3] Commonly called, " The Rabbling Act ". *Acts of Parliament of William III*, Sect. 5, c. 22.

throughout the north of Scotland. In addition to these activities, Episcopal meeting-houses were frequently mobbed, and Bishops and other clergy were often in danger of suffering violence.

On Queen Anne's accession to the throne in 1702, Episcopal clergy presented a " Humble Address and Supplication " to Her Majesty calling attention to the deplorable condition of the former National Church since the suppression of its ancient Apostolic government and the disgrace that many ordained for the service of Christ were being driven forth as wanderers to beg their bread. The Queen replied that while they observed the laws they should be protected in the exercise of their religion.[1]

When the General Assembly of 1703 complained that the Episcopal clergy were violating the laws of the land by baptizing, preaching, marrying, intruding into vacant churches, and despising sentences of deprivation, and proceeded to embody these complaints in an Act,[2] the Queen's commissioners abruptly dissolved the meeting.

A bill of toleration for all Protestant dissenters from the Established Church was introduced before the last of the Scottish Parliaments in 1703, but it was opposed by a remonstrance from the Commission of the General Assembly which stated:

" We do, therefore, most humbly beseech, yea, we are bold in the Lord, and in the name of the Church of God in this land earnestly to obtest that no such motion of any legal toleration to those of the prelatical principles be entertained by the Parliament; being persuaded that in the present case and circumstances of this Church and nation, to enact a toleration for those of that way would be to establish iniquity by a law, and would bring upon the promoters thereof, and upon their families, the dreadful guilt of all those sins, and pernicious effects both to Church and State, that may ensue thereupon."

Nothing more was heard of the bill.[3]

[1] Skinner, *History*, vol. 2, p. 601; Lawson, pp. 177–178.
[2] *Acts G.A.*, pp. 316–321.   [3] *Acts P.S.*, vol. 11, pp. 46–47.

Continuity of Episcopal Succession

It was realized by the Bishops that though the government of the Church might remain in its irregular condition for some time, it was their duty to provide for the preservation of the Episcopate and for the ordination of clergy. For fifteen years nothing was done to continue the episcopal succession, and vacancies in the Episcopate caused by death were left unfilled. When, however, in 1704, Archbishop Ross of St. Andrews, the Primate and Metropolitan, died, and only five of the Bishops in possession of sees at the Revolution were left, it became a matter of urgent concern what was to be done to maintain the succession. It was regarded as an infringement of the rights of " the king over the water " to appoint to vacant sees, and so no attempt was made to provide a successor to the late Primate or to fill any of the other vacant sees. The expedient adopted was to raise certain priests to the Episcopal Office without committing any particular dioceses to their rule. It was thought that such a plan would meet the needs of the Church while not interfering with the sovereign's privilege of nominating to vacant sees.[1]

Two worthy men, John Sage and John Fullarton, were chosen as the new Bishops. John Sage was ordained priest in the diocese of Glasgow in 1685, and three years later he was selected for the Professorship of Divinity at St. Mary's College, St. Andrews, though he was not permitted to occupy the chair on account of the Revolution. He officiated in one of the Edinburgh meeting-houses, though, on refusing to take the oath of allegiance and subscribe the assurance, he was compelled to return to Fife. He was a scholar and able apologist, and defended the Church strenuously and learnedly with his pen in these dark and anxious years. John Fullarton was a presbyter at Paisley at the Revolution, and had suffered the changes which had

---

[1] Grub, vol. 3, pp. 346–353.

fallen upon the Church. He became the first Primus of the Church.[1]

The new Bishops were consecrated on St. Paul's Day, January 25th, 1705, in an oratory in Archbishop Paterson's house in Edinburgh. The Archbishop of Glasgow and the Bishops of Edinburgh and Dunblane were the consecrators. The deaths of the Archbishop of Glasgow and the Bishop of Aberdeen made it necessary to consecrate two others in 1709. John Falconer and Henry Christie were selected and consecrated in Dundee. The Theological College in Edinburgh has in its keeping contemporary letters and documents which bear witness to these consecrations. The Bishops at the consecration of Falconer and Christie have been described as celebrating " with mournful privacy the most august solemnity of the Catholic Church ". Indeed these consecrations must have been charged with strong emotions as the newly selected candidates knelt before the worn old Bishops who were their consecrators to receive the Holy Ghost for the office and work of Bishops in the Church of God. On the death of Bishop Sage in 1711, Archibald Campbell, a Non-Juror, who continued to reside in England after his consecration, was made Bishop at Dundee by the Bishops of Edinburgh and Dunblane and Bishop Falconer.[2] Another presbyter consecrated Bishop at this time was James Gadderar, formerly minister at Kilmacolm in the Glasgow diocese. He was consecrated in London by Bishop Hickes, an English Non-Juring Bishop, and Bishops Falconer and Campbell, thus still further strengthening the links between the Scottish Episcopalians and the English Non-Jurors.[3] This identification of the cause of Episcopacy in Scotland with that of the Non-Jurors in England was unfortunate, especially as these two Scottish Bishops later took part in several English consecrations.

---

[1] Keith, *Catalogue*, pp. 518–521; Skinner, *History*, vol. 2, pp. 602–603.
[2] Attested copy of Deed of Consecration, P.E.C.S.; Keith, *Catalogue*, p. 530.
[3] Deed of Consecration, P.E.C.S.; Keith, *Catalogue*, p. 531.

The Worship of the Church

Soon after the Revolution efforts were made to restore liturgical services to the Church, and the model generally adopted was that of the English Book of Common Prayer.[1]   This practice roused the fiery wrath of the General Assembly of the Presbyterian Church, which passed a special Act in 1707 expressing their zeal for the uniformity of worship and especially their concern that certain ministers were apparently guilty of introducing innovations into public worship.   Further, the Act called upon all ministers to show to their people the evil of such innovations and to exhort them to beware of them.   The people were encouraged to deal with the innovators, and in particular to report them to the Presbyteries.[2]   The Commission of the Assembly was instructed to use every proper means by applying to the Government, or in any other way, for suppressing and removing all these innovations.

While justified in preventing their own ministers from practising and encouraging such innovations in public worship, the Assembly went beyond this and sought to hinder the use of liturgical services in Episcopal meeting-houses.   One illustration will suffice to show the attitude of the Presbyterian Establishment to the attempt to restore liturgical services in the Episcopal Church.

[1] Dr. Monro, Principal of the College of Edinburgh, was charged in 1690 with using the Book of Common Prayer in the College.   He stated that the Prayer Book had been used in the Chapel Royal in the reign of Charles I, and in many families since the Restoration (Grub, vol. 3, pp. 319, 358).   During the reign of Queen Anne there was a marked revival of liturgical worship throughout the Church.   So popular had the Prayer Book services become that a new edition of Laud's Liturgy was published in Edinburgh in 1712.   The generous charity of many well-disposed friends in the Church of England, especially in the University of Oxford, was expressed in the gift of above 19,000 Prayer Books and other devotional books in the space of two years prior to 1718.   There is evidence of the use of the Prayer Book in churches, as, for example, in the church of James Gordon at Banchory-Devenick (Somerville, *History of the Reign of Queen Anne*, p. 468; Don, *Scottish Book of Common Prayer*, p. 21; *A Representation of the State of the Church in North Britain*, p. 19; Sinclair, *Statistical Account of Scotland*, vol. 11, p. 181).

[2] *Acts G.A.*, p. 418.

James Greenshields, a native of Scotland, who was ordained priest by the deprived Bishop of Ross, returned to his native land in 1709, after holding several curacies in Ireland. He took the oath to the government and opened a place of worship, in which he used the services of the Church of England. He was summoned before the Presbytery of Edinburgh, but protested that he was not subject to their jurisdiction and could not accept any judgement they might pronounce. The Presbytery disregarded his plea and prohibited him from preaching, on the grounds that he declined their jurisdiction, that he exercised his ministry without their authority, and that he used innovations in public worship. The magistrates upheld this decision, and forbade Greenshields to preach on pain of imprisonment. He disregarded the order and officiated as usual on the following Sunday. He was consequently apprehended and committed to jail, where he remained for some time, having remitted the matter to the Lords of Session for their judgement, with the petition that qualified Episcopal clergy in Scotland ought to have as full liberty of worship according to their forms as Scottish Presbyterian ministers enjoyed in Ireland. The Court of Session refused his petition, but Greenshields appealed for redress to the British House of Peers, which reversed their judgement.[1]

The Act of Toleration

To prevent the recurrence of such proceedings against the Episcopal clergy in Scotland, a Bill was introduced into the House of Commons in 1712 and passed that House by a large majority. Its passage through the House of Lords was more difficult, but it received the royal assent in March of that year. The title of the Act is, " An Act to prevent the disturbing of those of the Episcopal Communion, in that part of Great Britain called Scotland, in the exercise of their religious worship, and in the use of

[1] Wodrow, *Correspondence*, vol. 1, pp. 68–69; Lathbury, *History of the Non-Jurors*, pp. 450–454; Chambers, vol. 3, p. 350.

the Liturgy of the Church of England; and for repealing the Act passed in the Parliament of Scotland, intituled ' An Act against irregular Baptisms and Marriages '.'' It asserted that it is free and lawful for Episcopalians in Scotland to meet for the exercise of divine worship, to be performed after their own manner by pastors ordained by a Protestant Bishop, and who are not established ministers of any church or parish, and to use in their congregations the Liturgy of the Church of England, if they think fit, without hindrance or disturbance. It was required, however, that Presbyterian ministers and Episcopal clergy alike must take the oaths of allegiance and abjuration, and pray, during divine service, for the Queen's Majesty, the Princess Sophia of Hanover, and all the royal family.

The conditions of the Toleration Act were accepted by many of the Episcopal clergy, but most of the Non-Jurors refused to sacrifice their political principles. A number of Aberdeen clergy under the leadership of Dr. James Garden and Dr. George Garden presented an address of congratulation to the Queen on the signing of the Peace of Utrecht, in which they acknowledged with thankfulness their freedom to exercise pastoral care over their people and in the use of the Liturgy of the Church of England.[1]

The State of the Church

One of the results of the Toleration Act was that clergy were able to continue their efforts for the introduction of liturgical worship both in those parish churches where the old incumbents remained and in the meeting-houses.

In the twenty-five years which had passed since the Church was disestablished and disendowed, most of the Bishops had died. The leader of those who remained was Bishop Rose of Edinburgh, he who had represented the Scottish Episcopate in the

[1] Grub, vol. 3, pp. 363–365; *Acts G.A.*, pp. 467–475; *Parliamentary History of England*, vol. 6, pp. 1126–1129.

interview with William, Prince of Orange. Certain priests had been consecrated Bishops but without the responsibilities of diocesan jurisdiction. Two of these Bishops resided in England and were closely identified with the English Non-Jurors. It would seem that the Bishops still waited hopefully for the return of the Stuart Kings and the restoration of the Church as the Established Church.

Nevertheless, the Act of Toleration ought to have opened the way for fuller and freer development of the life of the Church, and it would seem that many of the clergy, especially those who accepted the conditions of the Act and including the Aberdeen clergy who were led by James and George Garden, hoped that their new freedom would give them the opportunities of which they had been so long deprived. One might have expected to record the development of Episcopal oversight and the extension of the chain of meeting-houses, for it would seem that the influence of the disestablished Church was steadily increasing amongst the people of Scotland, but the death of Queen Anne in 1714 introduced an epoch of political intrigue and war which grievously injured the life of the Church.

5

THE JACOBITE REVOLT OF 1715 AND ITS EFFECTS ON THE CHURCH

The Insurrection

THE accession of King George I as King of Great Britain provided the occasion for a formidable revolt of Jacobite adherents in Scotland in favour of the son of the last Stuart King. In the autumn of 1715 the greater part of the kingdom beyond the Forth was in the possession of the insurgents. James, however, who joined the armies at the end of the year, was not an inspiring leader, and the dissensions already manifest amongst his officers made effective action difficult. The revolt was quickly controlled by the royal army, and many prisoners of high rank were executed.

Much evidence was available of the active part taken by Episcopal clergy in the insurrection. And so, in punishing the insurgents, the Government were impelled to renew proceedings against such clergy.

In May 1716 the King wrote to the Lords of Justiciary saying that he had been advised that there were meeting-houses in Edinburgh and elsewhere in Scotland in which prayers were not offered for himself and the royal family during divine service, and enjoining that such meeting-houses be closed and proceedings be instituted against the offenders.[1] The crown lawyers prepared indictments against the offending clergy in Edinburgh and district for not registering their Letters of Orders and for not praying for King George and the royal family. All except one

---

[1] Arnot, *Criminal Trials*, pp. 343–346.

were unable to produce Letters of Orders and were prohibited from officiating until this was done. Twenty-one were fined for not praying for the King. The clergy subsequently registered their Letters of Orders and were permitted to officiate as before.[1]

Episcopal clergy in the diocese of Aberdeen were particularly active in their support of the Stuart cause. A number of these clergy were still in possession of the parish churches, and several used the Book of Common Prayer in public worship. Most of the meeting-houses were closed, and the Presbyterians exploited the situation to have the Episcopal clergy ejected from the parish churches by the magistrates with the assistance of soldiers. Thirty-six clergy were thus deprived in the Aberdeen diocese and, for the first time, the University of Aberdeen was brought into conformity with the Established Presbyterian Church.[2]

The Abjuration Act

Following representations from the General Assembly, an Act was passed at Westminster in 1719 which enacted that no person should be permitted to officiate in any Episcopal meeting-house or congregation where nine or more persons were present, in addition to the members of the household, without praying for King George and the royal family, and without having taken the oath of abjuration, as required in the Toleration Act of 1712. The penalty prescribed was six months' imprisonment for the clergyman and the shutting up of his meeting-house for the same period.

Some of the clergy suffered under this statute, but its provisions were seldom enforced after the threat of invasion had

---

[1] Chambers, vol. 3, p. 405. The Toleration Act of 1712 had virtually granted to Episcopalians in Scotland the same toleration which Dissenters enjoyed in England. It had required that all clergy must register their Letters of Orders.

[2] *Historical Papers relating to the Jacobite Period*, Spalding Club, vol. 1; Grub, vol. 3, pp. 374–378; Wodrow, *Correspondence*, vol. 2, p. 210.

passed. Several congregations, however, decided to appoint clergy willing to take the oaths and who were thus "qualified" to officiate according to the English rite. One of the consequences of this decision was that clergy who "qualified" were generally outside the jurisdiction of the Scottish Bishops, who refused to sanction the ministrations of those who took the oaths to the reigning sovereign.[1]

Selection and Consecration of Bishops

Bishops Rose, Fullarton, and Falconer consecrated Arthur Millar and William Irvine to the Episcopate at the end of 1718.[2] When Bishop Rose died early in 1720 the last of the pre-Revolution Bishops passed from the scene, and the Episcopal Church was governed by four Bishops, resident in Scotland, having no diocesan jurisdiction. (Bishops Campbell and Gadderar were resident in England.) In effect, Bishop Rose was almost the sole ruler of the Church during the greater part of the period between the Revolution and his death in 1720. Though we may question the wisdom of his leadership because of his attachment to the House of Stuart, yet Bishop Rose remained faithful to the Church and was instrumental in preserving it from schism through the difficult years of persecution, while he took an important part in ensuring the continuity of the episcopal succession.[3]

None of the remaining Bishops possessed or claimed jurisdiction over the Church. They were not prepared to act independently, since they still believed that the right of nomination to the vacant sees rested with their exiled prince. However, a meeting of the Edinburgh clergy, attended by Bishops Falconer, Millar, and Irvine, resolved in 1720 to fill the vacant

[1] Grub, vol. 3, p. 378; W. Stephen, *History of the Scottish Church*, vol. 2, pp. 481–482.

[2] Bishop Millar's Deed of Consecration and an attested copy of Bishop Irvine's, P.E.C.S.; Keith, *Catalogue*, p. 526; Skinner, *History*, vol. 2, p. 621.

[3] Grub, vol. 3, p. 381; Keith, *Catalogue*, p. 65. Bishop Keith was a presbyter under Bishop Rose for seven years and described him as a "sweet-natured man".

see of Edinburgh and that all the clergy should have an equal voice in the election. Owing to the absence of the senior Bishop, Bishop Fullarton, the meeting was postponed till he could attend. At the resumed meeting, Bishop Fullarton produced on behalf of the Bishops their deeds of consecration and stated that they had been consecrated to preserve the succession but that they claimed no jurisdiction over any district. At a later meeting, attended by the clergy only [1] (about fifty of them), Bishop Fullarton was elected Bishop of Edinburgh. The other Bishops ratified the election and, assuming the title of " The Episcopal College ", they appointed the newly elected Bishop to be their president, with the title of Primus, but without any metropolitan jurisdiction. The theory was that the College of Bishops exercised metropolitan jurisdiction.[2]

The Bishops were still far too strongly bound up with the Jacobite cause, so that they appeared to be content merely to continue the succession, depending entirely on the voluntary recognition and support of the clergy and laity, without exercising their proper pastoral oversight over the Church. Thus, though the decisions about the oversight of the Edinburgh clergy and the forming of the Episcopal College with a Primus were taken by the clergy of the Edinburgh district and by the Bishops themselves, yet these decisions must be reported to the Chevalier, through his trustees in Scotland, so that he might give them his royal approbation. James replied approving of the promotions but requesting that in future the names of the persons proposed should be intimated to him for his consideration and previous sanction.[3]

A large body of the clergy of Angus and St. Andrews requested

---

[1] It would have been a hopeful sign if this opportunity had been taken to give the laity a voice in the election of the Bishops. The Church's restoration was, however, subordinated to the " rights " of the exiled prince.

[2] Skinner, *History*, vol. 2, p. 628; Lawson, p. 520.

[3] Lockhart, *Papers*, vol. 2, pp. 35–42; Letter from Bishop Falconer to Bishops Campbell and Gadderar, dated 3 May 1720, P.E.C.S.

that Bishop Falconer should assume spiritual superintendence over them, and this arrangement was carried out. In Aberdeen, however, clergy and laity sought permission to proceed to the election of a Bishop, but the person proposed, Dr. George Garden, was not acceptable to the College of Bishops, who suggested that there was no need for a new consecration if the clergy would agree to accept one of the present Bishops. Bishop Campbell was then chosen, but the College did not approve, on account of his advocacy of certain liturgical practices. Holding himself canonically elected, Bishop Campbell sent his friend, Bishop Gadderar, as his vicar while he remained in London. On the resignation of Bishop Campbell in 1725, Bishop Gadderar assumed the office of Bishop of the Aberdeen district.[1]

Andrew Cant, son of the Principal of the Edinburgh College and one of the ministers of Edinburgh before the Revolution, and David Freebairn, formerly minister at Dunning, were consecrated Bishops in Edinburgh in 1722.[2] Alexander Duncan and Robert Norrie were consecrated in 1724, and James Rose and John Ochterlonie were consecrated in 1726. Bishop Duncan exercised pastoral oversight in the Glasgow diocese, and Bishop Norrie superintended the congregations in Angus and Mearns.[3]

On the death of Bishop Fullarton in 1727 the clergy of Edinburgh elected Bishop Millar as their diocesan, and the Bishop of Aberdeen and Bishop Cant acknowledged him as Primus and also as Metropolitan, but the other Bishops refused to sanction the election.

Dr. Rattray was chosen by the clergy of Angus and Mearns to succeed Bishop Norrie, and he was consecrated at Edinburgh with the title of Bishop of Brechin. William Dunbar was chosen by the clergy of Moray and Ross and consecrated Bishop. Robert

---

[1] Skinner, op. cit., p. 629; *Scottish Eccles. Journal*, vol. 3, pp. 31, 58.
[2] The Deeds of Consecration of Bishops Cant and Freebairn, P.E.C.S.
[3] Bishop Duncan's Deed of Consecration, P.E.C.S.; Skinner, op. cit., p. 642; Grub, vol. 3, p. 395.

Keith became coadjutor Bishop of Edinburgh, and John Gillan and David Ranken were also consecrated Bishops.[1]

Though no claim was made by the Bishops to diocesan jurisdiction, the Bishops of Edinburgh were generally regarded as holding presidential authority within the College. This suited the purpose of James, who generally regarded the Primus as his ecclesiastical representative. James was not concerned with the needs and welfare of the Church but rather with his hopes of exercising his sovereignty.

At the same time, the Bishops were concerned not merely to maintain the continuity of the succession but also to provide for the superintendence of clergy and congregations in districts, as, for example, in the districts of Edinburgh, Aberdeen, Brechin, and Glasgow. This situation was in many ways unsatisfactory, for some Bishops of the College were responsible for the superintendence of districts and some had no such responsibilities. It thus became clear that the Bishops would have to decide whether they ought to remain bound by the restrictions imposed on their activities by the King they acknowledged or whether they ought more effectively to assume responsibility for the Church and appoint to each Bishop of the College an area for his supervision.

The Usages

The liturgical practices known as the Usages were chiefly the mixing of water with the wine at the Offertory, the commemoration of the faithful departed, the use of an express prayer of invocation, and the use of a formal prayer of oblation, all of these at the Eucharist. There were also such practices as immersion in Baptism and the use of consecrated oil in Confirmation and in the anointing of the sick.

As noted in the last chapter, the disestablished Church sought to recover for itself its rightful liturgical heritage, and the

[1] Skinner, op. cit., pp. 643–645; Keith, *Catalogue*, p. 552.

clergy began to introduce the Prayer Book. Some used the English Book of Common Prayer, but some preferred the 1637 Liturgy, which gave support to the Usages.

The Bishops were divided amongst themselves on the question of the Usages. Some of them, like Bishops Campbell and Gadderar, who were both closely associated with the English Non-Jurors, and Bishop Falconer, defended the Usages on primitive authority. Dr. Rattray, a scholarly priest, who became Bishop, regarded these liturgical practices as necessary parts of the highest act of public Christian worship, and of divine appointment, " as being instituted by Christ Himself, or by His apostles, and by them delivered to the Catholic Church ". The other Bishops were so strongly opposed to the Usages that they sent a letter to clergy and laity against what they regarded as the most objectionable of the Usages, namely the mixed chalice and prayers for the dead.

Bishop Gadderar in Aberdeen showed himself so keenly in favour of the Usages that he not only practised them himself but also encouraged their use by the clergy of his diocese. After much controversy the Bishops agreed to five articles in " The First Concordate ", according to which Bishop Gadderar accepted a compromise to preserve peace and unity in the Church, promising that he would not insist upon introducing any of the Usages unless the Primus and the rest of his brethren saw reason to order otherwise.[1]

The Canons of 1727

During the course of the controversy over the Usages, the Episcopal College met in Edinburgh in 1722, at which meeting the agent of the Chevalier, Lockhart, was present. Bishop Gadderar was outspokenly independent in insisting that the Church had the right to settle the controversy without regard to

[1] Lockhart, vol. 2, pp. 94–99; Skinner, op. cit., pp. 630–632; Grub, vol. 3, pp. 387–396, quoting MS. Memoirs of the Episcopal Church, P.E.C.S.

any external authority, but most of the other Bishops, nominees of James, were clearly unwilling to act on their own initiative without recourse to the exiled King. Again in 1724, when, at a meeting of the College discussing the choice of a Bishop for Angus and Mearns, exception was taken to the proposed selection of Bishop Norrie, since the majority of the clergy and laity preferred Dr. Rattray, Lockhart declared that the right of episcopal appointments belonged to the exiled King and that in future the royal prerogative would be exercised. The meeting broke up without a decision, but later the College of Bishops appointed Bishop Norrie to the district, though the Primus was instructed by James that in future no Bishop should be assigned to a district without his consent.

This situation was intolerable, and the clergy of the Edinburgh diocese did not hesitate to say so when the question arose of the choice of a Bishop for their district. In a remonstrance to the Episcopal College, they called upon the Bishops to recover the ancient rights of the Church to self-government and accused James of violating his engagements to the Bishops by the manner of his appointments.[1] Soon after this, Lockhart was obliged to seek safety at Rotterdam, since the Government had discovered that he was corresponding with the Chevalier. It was clear that the Church must decide for itself matters affecting the administration of the dioceses and questions about the selection of the Bishops and their jurisdiction. One of the difficult questions was to determine the future of the Episcopal College, especially as it concerned those Bishops of the College who had no jurisdiction.[2]

The groundwork of the Code of Canons by which the Episcopal Church in Scotland is still governed was provided by the Diocesan Bishops who met in Edinburgh in 1727 and framed six Canons. The Bishops in attendance were the Bishop of Edinburgh as Primus, and the Bishops of Aberdeen, Brechin, and Moray.

---

[1] Lockhart, vol. 2, p. 325.
[2] Grub, vol. 3, pp. 396–399.

Their aim was to establish a strictly diocesan Episcopacy with a Metropolitan.

The first Canon urged that all orders of clergy should regard the Bishop of Edinburgh as Metropolitan until the see of St. Andrews was restored.

The second Canon noted that councils of Bishops were intended chiefly for deliberation upon and regulating the affairs of the flock of Christ committed to them, and, therefore, that only Bishops with such a charge committed to them by the election of the clergy of a district, and confirmed by the Metropolitan with the consent of the other Bishops, were entitled to vote in these councils.

The third Canon described the practice of consecrating Bishops without jurisdiction as contrary to the Canons and practice of the Church and declared that no one, henceforth, was to be consecrated Bishop unless elected to a particular diocese by the majority of the presbyters of it, and that such consecration was to be performed by the Metropolitan, or at his order, with the consent of the other Bishops.

The fourth Canon commended the appointment, by the Bishop, of a Dean in each diocese whose duty was to superintend the election of a Bishop during a vacancy.

The fifth Canon prohibited any Bishop from performing any episcopal function in the diocese of another Bishop without his consent.

The sixth Canon required the subscription of every Bishop-elect to these Canons before his consecration.[1]

The Diocesan and the College Bishops

The Diocesan Bishops were concerned further to reach an agreement with their brethren, the College Bishops or the Bishops without jurisdiction, and they proposed an accommodation. The terms of the accommodation were that Bishop Millar

---

[1] Skinner, op. cit., p. 644; MS. Memoirs, P.E.C.S., p. 13.

be acknowledged Bishop of Edinburgh, in whom, during the vacancy of St. Andrews, the metropolitan powers be vested; that only Bishops with diocesan jurisdiction might vote on matters concerning the flock of Christ; but that the Diocesan Bishops continue to maintain correspondence with the other Bishops, to call them to meetings and to seek their advice, and in due course to welcome them to a decisive vote in matters relating to the well-being of the Church whenever any of them were elected and confirmed to the charge of dioceses.

The College Bishops continued to resist such proposals and declared that the Diocesan Bishops had no power or jurisdiction over the Scottish Church. However, the influence of the Diocesan Bishops increased steadily, and in due course conferences were held to prepare the way for an agreement, which was duly accepted in December 1731 by the Bishops of the Church in Scotland, and thus paved the way for a better administration of the affairs of the Church. The Agreement contained six articles: (1) that the Scottish or English Liturgy was to be used in public worship and no other and that the Usages were not to be observed; (2) that no man was to be consecrated a Bishop without the consent of the other Bishops; (3) that the election of a Bishop by the presbyters of any diocese was to be only on a mandate from the Primus with the consent of the other Bishops; (4) that the Bishops were to elect their Primus by a majority of votes, for the purpose of convening and presiding only; (5) that Bishop Freebairn was to be the Primus, and that the ten Bishops were to be responsible for the supervision of ten districts or dioceses without claiming any legal title to dioceses.[1]

The Canons of 1743

The difficulties which arose over elections to vacant sees and questions about the authority of the Bishops rendered necessary

[1] MS. Memoirs, P.E.C.S., pp. 16, 36; Lawson, appendix, p. 532; Skinner, op. cit., pp. 645–647; Chambers, vol. 3, p. 621; Letter from Bishop Keith to Bishop Rattray, December 4th, 1731, P.E.C.S.

the preparation of a number of Canons. It also appears evident that the Church was once again establishing itself in many centres throughout Scotland. There had been no attempt to provide a comprehensive Code of Canons since the effort of Charles I in 1636. The Bishops seemed to think the time propitious, and in 1743 they assembled in Synod at Edinburgh and unanimously adopted sixteen Canons for the government of the Church. The preamble to the Code of Canons reads: " The Bishops of the Church of Scotland being now, by the good providence of God, perfectly united in one and the same mind, and the concordates, that were formed while some unhappy differences subsisted amongst them, thereby vacated, they have unanimously agreed to establish the following Canons for the future regulation of the government of this Church."

The following notes summarize the Canons of 1743:

Primus. The Bishops are to select a Primus, by a majority of votes, without regard to seniority of consecration or precedency of district, but the duties of the Primus are limited to those of convening and presiding. He is liable to suspension from his office and from Episcopal jurisdiction in his own diocese if he lays claim to any further power than that granted by the Canons. He holds office only during the pleasure of the other Bishops.

Election of Bishops. Presbyters of the diocese are given the right to elect their Bishop, but they must wait till they receive a mandate from the Primus with the consent of the other Bishops or of the majority of the Bishops. Each Bishop is to appoint a Dean in his diocese, whose duty it is to apply for a mandate in the event of a vacancy in the see. If the clergy elect a consecrated Bishop, he is to have no jurisdiction until the election is confirmed by the majority of the Bishops, and if someone is chosen who is not acceptable to the majority of the Bishops a new election will be required. No one is to be consecrated a Bishop without the consent of the majority of the Bishops.

The Authority of the Bishops.   No presbyter may take charge of any congregation without the appointment of the Bishop of the diocese, and no one is to be ordained without a designation to a particular charge.   The Bishops are to urge clergy and ordinands to be diligent students of the Scriptures, and of the Fathers of the apostolic and next two ages, that the people may be instructed " in the truly Catholic principles of that pure and primitive church ".   If a presbyter or deacon deposed by his Bishop presumes to gather a separate or schismatical congregation, he is to be excommunicated, and laity who follow such a person are forbidden to partake of church ordinances unless received by the Bishop after reconciliation.

A Bishop who has charge of a congregation in a diocese other than his own is exempt from the jurisdiction of the Bishop of that diocese, and his assistants in such a congregation are to be under his jurisdiction.

Episcopal Synods.   The Primus is allowed a casting vote in the case of an equality of votes in Synod.   No Synod can be held unless the majority of the Bishops are present, though a Bishop unable to attend the Synod may send his judgement, on any matter previously advertised, by writing, and this is to be accepted for his canonical vote.   Deans are now allowed to attend Episcopal Synods but without the right of voting, though they may take part in discussions.

Other Matters.   Penalties are detailed against clergy who perform the marriage service over persons of another congregation without a recommendation from their former pastor.

The senior Bishop is given authority to succeed to the power of the Primus, in the event of his death, until the Episcopal Synod appoints a new Primus.

During a vacancy in any diocese, clergy are advised to apply to the nearest Bishop for the performance of Episcopal duties.

The Bishops also agreed at the Synod to recommend the use of the Scottish Liturgy in the administration of the Holy Communion and that none should be admitted to the Communion until confirmed by the Bishop or desirous of being confirmed.[1]

The clergy of the Edinburgh diocese sent a long and carefully reasoned reply to the Bishops objecting to the enactment of the Canons by the sole authority of the Bishops, who had made no attempt to hear the voice of the clergy and to receive their consent. They claimed a right to share in all ecclesiastical legislation and asserted that in the ancient Church of Scotland " presbyters did sit in Synods and Church Assemblies with their Bishops, not barely to hear and propose, but to reason and represent; that they had authoritative voices, and voted decisively, in whatsoever question came before them ". Several of the provisions of the Canons also occasioned dissatisfaction amongst the Edinburgh clergy, but elsewhere there does not appear to have been any widespread opposition to the new Code of Canons.[2]

Though the Canons of 1743 represent a distinct advance in the direction of constitutional Episcopal government, yet the Bishops seemed even then to be acting merely for a temporary period, for in an annexed declaration they stated that they did not arrogate to themselves any temporal right or regulation of districts, or seek to encroach upon the rights and privileges of the competent secular powers. Indeed, it would seem that they still waited for and expected the restoration of the legal establishment of the Church.

Soon, however, the country was in the throes of another dynastic insurrection.

The State of the Church

During the fifty-five years since the Revolution, years of persecution and dissension, the numbers of clergy and people had

[1] Minutes of the Synod of 1743, P.E.C.S.; MS. Memoirs, p. 24; Skinner, op. cit., pp. 654–660.
[2] MS. Memoirs, p. 25; Lawson, pp. 269–276, quoting from a MS. in the Faculty of Advocates, " Disputes of the Episcopalians ".

steadily diminished. On the eve of the Forty-five rebellion, there were probably less than one hundred and fifty clergy in communion with the Scottish Bishops. Yet in the period between the two Jacobite insurrections there are signs of developing life. Ample evidence of this may be found in the Canons themselves, for they reflect the need for more clearly defined regulations for the government of the Church through the Bishops within the districts assigned to them. It is not possible to assess the number of members of the Church throughout Scotland, but it has been suggested that in many districts of the north a majority of the middle and lower classes still adhered to Episcopacy.

The Church had greatly improved its order of worship, and it would appear that the Book of Common Prayer was in general use throughout the country. Further, several editions of the Scottish Liturgy had been printed and were extensively used. Bishop Keith stated that at this time most of the clergy, apart from those in the Edinburgh diocese, used the Scottish Communion Office, and it is significant that the Bishops agreed to recommend from their Synod of 1743 that the Scottish Liturgy be generally used in the administration of the Holy Communion. Clergy and laity seem to have been united in willing obedience to the Bishops and in attachment to the worship and doctrines of the Church.

The Church might have steadily regained its strength if the Bishops had continued to guide it as spiritual rulers and had disregarded all mere political considerations. In the summer of 1745, however, when Prince Charles Edward Stuart, grandson of James the Seventh, landed in Scotland, many Episcopalians rallied to his call and became involved in another insurrection.

6

THE INSURRECTION OF 1745 AND THE PENAL LAWS

The Forty-five Rebellion

A WAVE of Jacobite enthusiasm passed through the highlands of Scotland when the news was received that Prince Charles had landed to claim the ancestral throne. In the lowlands there was a strong feeling of antipathy to the Union with England, together with a ready manifestation of loyalty to the young prince who had so deeply committed himself to the fidelity of his Scottish subjects. Within a few weeks of the raising of his standard Charles was in possession of Edinburgh and defeated a Hanoverian army at Prestonpans. However, English support was not available to supplement the Scots forces; Charles was forced to retreat from Derby, and in the spring of 1746 his army was utterly defeated at Culloden.

The Duke of Cumberland, victor of Culloden, determined to teach the Scots the penalty of rebellion by inflicting upon them the severest humiliations. He carried out his policy of suppression with terrible effect. Under his orders, cottages, farm steadings, and villages, throughout the highlands, were razed to the ground, and many people were rendered homeless.[1]

The Episcopal Church Suppressed

Many Episcopalians were Jacobite at heart and wanted to see the restoration of the Stuart dynasty, but few of them openly committed themselves to supporting the rebellion. Of the

[1] Lecky, *History of England in 18th Cent.*, vol. 1, p. 423: "The Hanoverian army and the Duke of Cumberland displayed a barbarity which recalled the memory of Sedgemoor and of the Bloody Assize."

clergy, only two followed the army of Charles, and both were executed. Nevertheless, the Duke of Cumberland was determined to destroy the Episcopal chapels wherever he could find them, and his march north from the Tay to the Spey was notable for the number of Episcopal chapels which he destroyed. This policy of burning and destroying Episcopal chapels was continued with even greater severity after Culloden. Further, the Government were determined to increase the severity of the laws with the purpose of suppressing the ministrations of the Episcopal clergy, who were regarded as being largely responsible for the rebellion.[1]

In the summer of 1746 an Act was passed to prohibit and prevent pastors from officiating in Episcopal meeting-houses in Scotland without duly qualifying themselves according to the law, and also to punish any who resorted to meeting-houses where " unqualified " clergy officiated. This Act declared that all clergy of Episcopal congregations in Scotland must take the oaths appointed by the law before September the First, and thereafter must pray in public worship for the King and the royal family by name. All meeting-houses of which the clergy did not comply were to be shut up. Clergy who officiated after this date without having " qualified " were to be liable to imprisonment for six months for the first offence and transportation to the American colonies for life on the second or subsequent offence. A meeting-house, within the meaning of the Act, was defined as any meeting or congregation where five or more persons, in addition to the members of the family if in a house, or five or more persons where no family was residing, assembled for public worship performed by an Episcopal clergyman. Laity attending such prohibited meetings were liable to a fine of £5 for the first offence and imprisonment for two years for the second or subsequent offence. Other disabilities were imposed on peers, Members of Parliament, magistrates, or other public officers.

---

[1] Grub, vol. 4, pp. 35–37.

This Act also declared that only Letters of Orders given by a Bishop of England or Ireland would be deemed sufficient, or accepted for registration, after September the First. The obvious intention of this clause was to suppress the Scottish Episcopal Church and the native clergy and to grant toleration only to those who derived their orders from English or Irish Bishops.

Only five clergymen attempted to avail themselves of the provisions of this Act by " qualifying ", and these continued to officiate in meeting-houses. The public ministrations of all the other clergy who were in communion with the Scottish Bishops ceased, though many of these clergy continued to minister to small groups, sometimes offending against the law and suffering imprisonment accordingly. Many clergy and laypeople were transported to Barbados, especially from the north-east of Scotland, under the Penal Laws.[1]

Severe as the Act of 1746 was, the Government introduced a bill to Parliament in May 1748 declaring that no Letters of Orders, apart from those granted by Bishops of the Church of England or of Ireland, would be sufficient after September 1748 to " qualify " any clergyman to officiate. This new Act passed through the Commons with ease, but was resisted by a considerable minority in the Lords, including all the Bishops. Whereas the 1746 Act had meant that clergy ordained by Scottish Bishops would be accepted until September '46 but that after that date ordinands would have to seek ordination in England or Ireland, the 1748 Act " disqualified " all clergy ordained by Scottish Bishops, making it impossible for them to continue officiating anywhere except in their own houses. John Skinner, the minister of the Episcopal congregation at Longside in Aberdeenshire, had " qualified " in terms of the 1746 Act, but this was of no avail under the provisions of the 1748 Act.[2] A further

---

[1] T. Stephen, *History of the Church of Scotland*, vol. 4, pp. 327–329; ·MS. Memoirs, P.E.C.S., p. 30; *Parliamentary History*, vol. 14, pp. 269–315.
[2] MS. Memoirs, p. 32; Walker, *John Skinner of Linshart*, p. 46.

clause in this Act prohibited any clergyman, other than the ministers of the Established Church, from serving as a chaplain in any family in Scotland without taking the oaths.

Under these severe restrictions, it was difficult to administer the Church. Many clergy assembled their people in small numbers in their own houses at different times. Later, however, when the rigorous enforcement of the law abated, a number of expedients were adopted to keep within the letter of the law. For example, divine service was celebrated in one compartment where only the statutory number was present, but the house was so arranged that others in adjoining rooms could hear and see. Sometimes the people assembled in larger numbers in the woods and hills.

Public worship was inevitably grievously disorganized, and many irregularities became customary. Many who desired freedom of worship sought out the English " qualified " chapels which began to appear in a number of towns. At the same time a number of Scots postulants for ordination found their way into England and, after ordination there, returned to minister to their Episcopalian brethren in Scotland. Nevertheless, it was clearly impossible to secure a sufficient supply of pastors for the scattered flocks.[1]

The Continuity of the Episcopal Succession

In spite of these calamitous conditions, the Bishops did not neglect the duty of securing the continuance of the episcopal succession. On the death of Bishop Dunbar of Aberdeen, the clergy found means to elect as a successor one of themselves, Andrew Gerard, who was consecrated at Cupar, Fife, in 1747 by Bishops White, Falconer, Rait, and Alexander.[2] On the death

---

[1] Grub, vol. 4, pp. 41–46.
[2] MS. Register of the College of Bishops, vol. 1, p. 17; MS. Memoirs, p. 31; Skinner, *History*, vol. 2, p. 670; The Deeds of Consecration of Bishops Dunbar and Gerard, P.E.C.S.

of the Primus, Bishop Keith,[1] Bishop White was elected as his successor, and a coadjutor was chosen and consecrated in the person of Henry Edgar, a priest at Arbroath.

The State of the Church

The Penal Laws of George II had answered the purpose for which they were designed. The church was crippled, and the number of its laity had greatly decreased. There were very few clergy, and there was no opportunity for public worship except in the English " qualified " chapels, which were outside the jurisdiction of the Scottish Bishops.

Sir Walter Scott's description of the Church as " reduced to a mere shadow of a shade " describes the situation at the close of the reign of George II. Yet the Church was not left without witnesses. A picture, which has been reproduced as a poster and finds an honoured place in many Episcopal churches throughout Scotland at the present time, recalls a scene at Stonehaven wherein three clergymen of the district, Greig, Petrie, and Troup, shared the same cell because of their ministrations, which were declared to be against the law.[2] The picture depicts faithful churchpeople bringing their children to the clergy in their prison-tower for Baptism.

The Bishops could not in their enforced seclusion exercise much supervision over their clergy; indeed there is very little that can be said about the life of the Church at this time, since secrecy was imposed upon Episcopal and clerical ministrations everywhere because of the persecution. Yet the Church was

---

[1] When Episcopacy was in its most depressed condition Bishop Keith published his invaluable *Historical Catalogue of the Scottish Bishops*, to which reference is frequently made in these notes. He also published the first and only published volume of a *History of the Affairs of Church and State in Scotland* in 1734. A biography of Bishop Keith is prefixed to Bishop Russell's edition of the *Catalogue*.

[2] Walker, *Bishop Alexander Jolly*, p. 18.

being weaned from that alliance which had caused it so much distress, and the clergy were given opportunities of dreaming about the time when, restored to freedom, they might realize their duties to guide and govern the Church and to lead its people in worship in the form of its ancient Liturgy.

7

TOWARDS THE REPEAL OF THE PENAL LAWS
(1760–1792)

The Accession of George III

SOON after the accession of the young sovereign, George III, to the British throne, a favourable change took place in the fortunes of the Church. The new King had no desire to enforce the rigorous laws against Episcopalians in Scotland, and the awareness of this change of policy quickly influenced the clergy, who were able to discharge their pastoral duties more openly, and their congregations were encouraged in a humble way to erect buildings or lease premises for their proscribed worship. Many clergy and laity were ready to acknowledge the King in possession of the throne. Indeed, the cause of Jacobitism became little more than a name when the Chevalier died in 1766. It finally died, so far as Episcopalians were concerned, with the death of Charles Edward in 1788.

The Scottish Communion Office

The controversy over the Usages had prevented a more general adoption of the Scottish Communion Office until in 1743 the Bishops unanimously commended its use when they issued the Code of Canons. It is reasonable to suppose that the Scottish Liturgy was in general use so far as circumstances permitted, though with many irregularities, during the next fifteen years. Editions of the Liturgy had been published in 1735, 1743, and again in 1755, but it was thought that a revised edition should be prepared, and this was done under the supervision of the Primus and published in 1764. Thus we may rightly speak of the Scottish

Communion Office as the offspring of the Church in the days of her deepest depression and persecution. The model was the liturgy of the ill-fated 1637 book.

The order of the Communion Office is familiar to all who know the Scottish Liturgy in current use in the Province. The Offertory Prayer from 1 Chronicles 29 followed the Offertory Sentences and was followed by the *Sursum Corda*, the Proper Preface, the *Sanctus*, and the Prayer of Consecration, with the Oblation and Invocation after the Words of Institution. Then followed the Prayer for the Church without the words "militant here in earth" in the introduction, the Lord's Prayer, the Invitation to Communicants, the General Confession, the Absolution, the Comfortable Words, the Prayer of Humble Access, the Communion, the exhortation to Thanksgiving, the Thanksgiving, the *Gloria in Excelsis*, and the Blessing.

The sequence of the 1764 rite follows closely that of the Liturgy of St. Chrysostom. Bishops Campbell and Gadderar had shared with the English Non-Jurors in the preparation of the Non-Jurors' Office of 1718, and in plans to restore long-interrupted communion with the Eastern Orthodox Churches. During the controversy over the Usages, interpolations and changes in the order were freely made in the 1662 Communion Office, notably by Bishop Gadderar and many of his clergy. Bishop Rattray, who became Bishop of Dunkeld in 1731, laboured to commend the pattern of "The Ancient Church of Jerusalem", the Liturgy of St. James. The influence of Bishop Rattray's work can be recognized in Bishop Falconer's edition of the Scottish Communion Office, issued in 1755.[1] The groundwork had been well prepared, and the times were more favourable; in the words of Bishop Skinner: "In this favourable appearance of returning serenity it was thought proper to revise our Communion Office, and bring it, now that there was no contention or difference about it, to as exact a conformity

[1] Dowden, *The Annotated Scottish Communion Office*, pp. 97–107; Don, *Scottish Book of Common Prayer*; Grub, vol. 4, p. 87.

with the ancient standards of Eucharistic service as it would bear."[1] The exhortation to Thanksgiving, which first appears in the 1764 Office, is a modification of the bidding by the Deacon at the corresponding point in the Clementine Liturgy.

It is worthy of note that, in addition to its influence upon the worship of the Scottish Province through the succeeding generations, the 1764 Communion Office was taken to America by Bishop Seabury, who promised carefully to consider it and, if he found it agreeable to ancient practice, to sanction and encourage its use in his own diocese of Connecticut. Through this means of introduction, the Scottish Liturgy has greatly influenced the Communion Office of the American Church throughout its history.

The Restoration of Episcopal Supervision

An effort was made at this time to restore the administration of the Church through the Bishops, and several steps were taken to this end. When Bishop White died in 1761, his place as Primus was taken by Bishop Falconer of Moray, and his place as Bishop of the Fife district was taken by Bishop Edgar. So successful had been the persecution of the Church in the northern dioceses of Ross and Caithness that only one priest remained. Nevertheless, a presbyter of Leith, Robert Forbes, was consecrated Bishop of Ross and Caithness.

In 1776 the Primus, Bishop Falconer, transferred from Moray to Edinburgh, which had been without a Bishop for thirty-seven years. His place at Moray was taken by a priest at Folla, Arthur Petrie, who was duly consecrated Bishop. On the death of Bishop Forbes, Bishop Petrie added to his diocese the charge of Ross and Caithness. On the death of Bishop Gerard in 1767, the Aberdeen clergy elected Robert Kilgour, a priest at Peterhead, and he was consecrated Bishop. In 1774 Charles Rose became Bishop of Dunblane, and later, at the request of the clergy of Dunkeld, he added this diocese to his care.

[1] Dowden, p. 98.

In 1778 George Innes became Bishop of Brechin.

Bishop Falconer was succeeded as Primus by Bishop Kilgour of Aberdeen and a coadjutor was provided for the new Primus by the consecration of John Skinner. On the death of Bishop Falconer in 1784, there were five Scottish Bishops and only about forty other clergy; the Bishops were all in the northern areas of Scotland: Dunblane and Dunkeld, Brechin, Aberdeen, and Moray, Ross and Caithness.[1]

Consecration of Samuel Seabury

At this period when the fortunes of the Church seemed so low, the Scottish Bishops took part in an act which at once directed attention to their little struggling communion.

At the end of the war of American Independence in 1783, American churchmen were left in a state of ecclesiastical anarchy. The Church of England had never consecrated Bishops for the American Church in the colonial days. All ordinands in the colonies had been obliged to face the hazards of a trans-ocean voyage to secure ordination. On the restoration of peace it was realized in the American Church that unless they could obtain duly consecrated Bishops they would be swamped by the sects which were in existence around them. The laws of England, however, forbade anyone to be consecrated there who did not acknowledge the royal supremacy.

Clergy of Connecticut selected Samuel Seabury, one of their number, for the office of a Bishop and sent him to seek consecration at the hand of the English prelates. After the failure of his efforts in England, he was referred to the Scottish Bishops, to whom he applied in the following manner: '' I apply to the good Bishops in Scotland, and I hope I shall not apply in vain. If they consent to impart the Episcopal succession to the Church

---

[1] Keith, *Catalogue*, pp. 540–545; Skinner, *History*, vol. 2, pp. 683–697; *Scots Magazine*, vol. 37, p. 638, and vol. 46, p. 697; MS. Register of the College of Bishops, vol. 1, pp. 21–26, 31.

of Connecticut, they will, I think, do a great work, and the blessing of thousands will attend them. And, perhaps for this cause, among others, God's Providence has supported them, and continued their succession under various and great difficulties, that a free, valid, and purely ecclesiastical Episcopacy may from them pass into the western world."

The Scottish Bishops readily assented to the application, and Samuel Seabury was consecrated in a room in Aberdeen on November 14th, 1784, by the Primus, the Bishop of Moray and Ross, and the coadjutor Bishop of Aberdeen. On the following day, the Scottish Bishops and Bishop Seabury met in Synod and agreed to certain articles " to serve as a concordate or bond of union between the Catholic remainder of the ancient Church of Scotland and the new rising Church in Connecticut ".

The following is a brief summary of the Articles:

(1) To embrace the doctrines of the Gospel as revealed and set forth in the Holy Scriptures and to maintain the common faith once delivered to the saints.

(2) That the Church is the mystical body of Christ, of which He alone is the Head and Supreme Governor; and that the Bishops are under Him the chief ministers of this spiritual society, the exercise of their sacred office being independent of all lay powers.

(3) That the Episcopal Church in Connecticut is to be in full communion with the Episcopal Church in Scotland.

(4) That there should be as near a conformity in worship and discipline between the two churches as is consistent with differing circumstances and national customs.

(5) In particular, since the celebration of the Holy Eucharist is the principal bond of union among Christians, as well as the most solemn act of worship in the Christian Church, the Scottish Bishops commended the adoption of the Scottish Communion Office to the use of the Church of Connecticut, and Bishop Seabury agreed carefully to consider the Communion

Office and, if he found it agreeable to ancient practice, to sanction it and to introduce it by degrees by gentle methods of argument and persuasion in his diocese.

(6) Further, that a regular brotherly fellowship between the two Churches by a mutual intercourse of ecclesiastical correspondence be maintained.

(7) The Bishops concluded by saying that in the whole of this transaction " they have nothing else in view but the Glory of God, and the good of His Church ".

On his return to his American diocese, Bishop Seabury was warmly welcomed by his clergy, who presented to him an address which expressed their gratitude for his return and especially that now they were able to enjoy the long and ardently desired blessing of a pure, valid, and free Episcopacy.

The address recalled the previous attempts to gain this gift from the Church of England and the failure of these attempts, and then continued: " But, blessed be God, another door was opened for you. In the mysterious economy of His Providence, He had preserved the remains of the old Episcopal Church of Scotland under all the malice and persecutions of its enemies. In the school of adversity, its pious and venerable Bishops had learned to renounce the pomps and grandeur of the world, and were ready to do the work of their heavenly Father. And, wherever the American Church shall be mentioned in the world, may this good deed which they have done for us be spoken of for a memorial of them."

Bishop Seabury's reply to the address expressed pleasure at the feelings entertained towards the Scottish Bishops, and added, " Their conduct through the whole business was candid, frank, friendly and Christian, appearing to me to arise from a just sense of duty, and to be founded in, and conducted by, the true principles of the primitive Apostolic Church." [1]

---

[1] Wilberforce, *History of the American Church*, pp. 195–231; Skinner, *History*, vol. 2, pp. 683–687; *Sc. Eccles. Journal*, vol. 1, pp. 215–217; Grub, vol. 4,

Change of Primus and New Bishops

John Skinner succeeded Bishop Kilgour as Bishop of Aberdeen in 1786 and also as Primus in 1788. Andrew MacFarlane, a priest at Inverness, was consecrated coadjutor to Bishop Petrie of Moray, Ross, and Caithness, and soon afterwards, on his death, succeeded him as Bishop of this northern diocese.[1]

Bishop Petrie's house at Folla in the Aberdeen diocese was used as a Theological College for men intended for the ministry of the Church. One of his pupils, Bishop Jolly, later carried on the same work for the Church, and, since the Panton Trust was initiated by a bequest from a parishioner of Bishop Jolly's at Fraserburgh, we may thus trace a connecting link between the work of training men for the service of the ministry carried out by Bishop Petrie, and later by his pupil, Bishop Jolly, through the succeeding years to the work carried on in the present Theological College of the Province, of which the Principal is generally the Pantonian Professor of Theology.[2]

Dr. Drummond was elected and consecrated Bishop of Brechin in 1787, and John Strachan, a priest in Dundee, was consecrated his coadjutor. No one had been appointed to the see of Edinburgh after the death of Bishop Falconer in 1784, but soon after his consecration as Bishop of Brechin, Dr. Drummond became Bishop of Edinburgh and Bishop Strachan succeeded him at Brechin.

Bishop John Skinner

Bishop Skinner was the most able and statesmanlike of the Bishops and proved himself to be a great leader of the Church

---

pp. 91–98. Later, an Act of Parliament removed the legal obstacles, and William White and Samuel Provoost, two American presbyters elected as Bishops of Pennsylvania and New York, were consecrated at Lambeth in 1787.

[1] MS. Register of the College of Bishops, vol. 1, p. 47; Skinner, *The Annals of the Episcopal Church in Scotland*, p. 67.

[2] Walker, *Bishop Alexander Jolly*.

throughout his episcopate. His father was the priest referred to above who suffered imprisonment after the Forty-five, under the terms of the 1748 Act. The Bishop, who shared the imprisonment of his father when a lad and had lived through these years of adversity, came to take a leading part in the restoration of the Church's freedom. He was foremost in supporting the application of Samuel Seabury for consecration, and as coadjutor Bishop of Aberdeen he shared, as one of the consecrators, in transmitting the sacred gift of the Episcopate to the American Church.

In 1788 Charles Edward Stuart died, and Bishop Skinner, who had just become Primus, called an Episcopal Synod to be held at Aberdeen. As the 1743 Canons directed, the Deans were also invited as representatives of the clergy. The Synod resolved to give evidence of their submission to George III as their sovereign by praying for him in the words of the English Prayer Book, and instructions were issued to all the clergy accordingly. Notice of this decision was sent to the Secretary of State, that it might be communicated to the King, who duly acknowledged it.

Bishop Skinner now turned his attention to secure the abolition of the Penal Laws and both in his consultations in London and in his discussions in Scotland he was wonderfully patient and far-sighted. He was clearly a great leader and a wise guide, and was allowed to serve the Church as Primus for twenty-eight years till his death in 1816.

In addition to his great work as Bishop of Aberdeen and as Primus of the Scottish Church, it is worthy of note that John Skinner was the clergyman in charge of the Episcopal congregation which met in Longacre, in the room where Bishop Seabury was consecrated, for several years before he became a Bishop, and after that for some twenty years till his son, William, succeeded as incumbent. It was largely as a result of the exertions of Bishop Skinner that he was able in 1795 to lead his congregation from the room in Longacre to the Church of St. Andrew which they built, and which now serves as the Cathedral of the diocese of Aberdeen and Orkney.

This account of John Skinner as parish priest, Bishop, and, at the beginning of his work, as Primus, introduces us to the important events which freed the Church from the Penal Laws.[1]

The Repeal of the Penal Laws

Early in 1789, one hundred years after the Revolution, Bishop Skinner as Primus, Bishop Drummond of Edinburgh and Bishop Strachan of Brechin went off to London to appeal to the Government for relief from the oppressive laws which had so effectively crippled their Church. The Bishops were pleased with the reception they received from the Primate and several of the English Bishops. A paper was prepared by Sir James Allan Park, dealing with the case of the Episcopal clergy and laity in Scotland, which recalled the terms of the Toleration Act and the Penal Statutes and concluded with a petition for the repeal of these laws. A bill was then introduced into the House of Commons on the lines of the petition and was passed without any opposition. In the House of Lords, however, the Chancellor moved its adjournment on grounds which have not been explained.

The Primus and his brother Bishops returned to Scotland and called a convention of clergy and lay representatives to meet at Laurencekirk so that they might learn of the proposals made for the repeal of the Penal Laws and might offer advice. As a result of the convention, a joint committee of three Bishops, three clergy, and three laymen was appointed, with full power to take further measures to obtain the repeal. In due course the application was renewed and both Houses of Parliament passed an amended bill for the repeal of the Penal Laws, and the royal assent on June 15th, 1792, granted relief to the Episcopal clergy by permitting them to minister to their people.

The Repeal Act required that all Scottish Episcopal clergy

[1] Walker, *Bishop John Skinner*.

must subscribe the oath of allegiance and the oath of abjuration, assent to the Thirty-nine Articles of the Church of England, and pray for the royal family during public worship. A disabling clause declared that such clergy should be incapable of holding any benefice, curacy, or other spiritual preferment in England or of officiating in England unless ordained by an English or Irish Bishop.[1]

A further convention at Laurencekirk was addressed by Primus Skinner on the Repeal Act on his return to Scotland. He expressed regret at the imposition of the oath of abjuration, though he was not greatly concerned at any other clauses. As to the disability, he remarked that the Church in Scotland had no other object but the promotion of true religion and " ought to have none else for its ministers but those who expect their reward in a better country than England, and from a Master whose kingdom is not of this world ". He suggested that the Church in Scotland should adopt the Thirty-nine Articles as its own to avoid the anomaly of one Church being required to subscribe the Articles of another. The meeting unanimously approved of all that had been done in connexion with the Repeal Act.[2]

The State of the Church

Though sadly reduced in numbers and with only four Bishops and a few clergy, its churches only a few poor meeting-houses, and its material resources lamentably small, yet the Church of 1792 was ready to rise to the opportunities provided in the repeal of the Penal Laws, and it was led, under God the Holy Spirit, by an able and faithful Bishop in Primus Skinner. Through the fires of persecution and adversity, its Bishops had learned the lesson that they were the spiritual pastors of the Church, bearing on behalf of their divine Head and Supreme Governor the charge

[1] *Parliamentary History*, vol. 24, pp. 1363–1373; Stanhope, *Life of Pitt*, vol. 1, p. 225.
[2] Skinner, *Annals*, pp. 233, 245–254.

and jurisdiction of the flock of Christ, and exercising their sacred office independently of secular patronage.

The Church possessed a " pure, valid, and free Episcopacy ", but there was need for some opportunity to be given to clergy and laypeople to take their full part in the administration of the affairs of the Church. Only step by step, as the nineteenth century moved on its course, were clergy admitted to their rightful place in the government of the Church and not till the third quarter of the century were lay representatives of congregations given an effective voice in administration.

There had developed a system of diocesan jurisdiction which corresponded to the needs of the time, though it required supplementing and adjustment to the needs of the Church as the latter extended its work in the Province and developed to fuller vitality. In connexion with all this, the clergy had acquired and had learned to exercise the right to choose their chief pastor.

The Canons of 1743 needed careful revision. Relief from the Penal Laws gave opportunity for important discussions on the alterations and additions that were called for.

In the first rank of the priceless possessions of the Church of 1792 must be set the Scottish Communion Office. Dr. Williams, a successor to Bishop Seabury in the diocese of Connecticut, is reported to have said that " in giving the primitive form of consecration [of the Eucharist], Scotland gave us a greater boon than when she gave us the Episcopate "

There were a number of " qualified " chapels, where clergy of English or Irish ordination ministered, but these owed no allegiance to the Scottish Bishops. An effort would be made to unite with them. There was also need to prepare plans for the development of existing congregations and the launching of new ventures.

The year of the repeal of the Penal Laws marks the beginning of a new chapter in the life of the Church, a chapter of many difficulties and problems and many opportunities.

8

" SETTING THE HOUSE IN ORDER "

The Qualified Chapels

THE Primus had much at heart the restoration to the unity of the Church of those congregations of churchpeople who were outside the jurisdiction of the Scottish Bishops. The repeal of the Penal Laws and the acknowledgement of the House of Hanover removed the causes of separation. One or two congregations had already placed themselves under the Scottish Bishops, but the majority of them kept apart. Most of these congregations were situated in the Edinburgh region, and the Primus thought that an end to the schism might be effected by the elevation to the Bishopric of Edinburgh of a priest of English ordination, Jonathan Boucher. The scheme was at first welcomed, but when it was reported that its purpose was to introduce Bishops into Scotland with the sanction of the Government, some members of the Established Church and other dissenting bodies stirred up an agitation which excited suspicion in the Qualified Chapels themselves. In these circumstances, Jonathan Boucher declined to proceed further.[1]

It became clear to the Primus that the only way to bring back the separated congregations was the adoption of the Thirty-nine Articles, and to this end, with the approval of his colleagues, he summoned a convocation of the clergy to meet together at Laurencekirk in 1804. Bishop Jolly addressed the convocation with a summary of the history of the Articles and their interpretation in relation to the errors against which they were directed. After some discussion the assembled clergy then agreed to subscribe the Thirty-nine Articles, with regard to which they

[1] Skinner, *Annals*, pp. 265–270.

declared that, after serious consideration of their obligation for the preservation of truth, unity, and concord in their Church and having observed with regret that no public Confession of Faith had been prescribed or handed down to them, " It would be highly expedient to exhibit some public testimony of our agreement in doctrine and discipline with the united Church of England and Ireland and to give a solemn declaration of our assent to her Thirty-nine Articles of Religion." Further, " we do acknowledge all and every the Articles contained therein, being in number Thirty-nine, besides the ratification, to be agreeable to the word of God. And we, the subscribing Bishops have also resolved in future to require from all candidates for Holy Orders in our Church, previously to their being ordained, a similar subscription." [1]

The Bishops then made overtures to the clergy of separated congregations, asking them to agree with their people to become pastors and members of the Church in Scotland, of which the Scottish Bishops are the regular governors. They submitted certain articles, of which the following is a summary.

Every clergyman was asked to submit his Letters of Orders to the Bishop of the diocese in which he was settled, so that they might be authenticated and registered, and declare his assent to the whole doctrine of the Gospel as revealed and set forth in the Scriptures, and acknowledge that the Scottish Episcopal Church is a pure and orthodox part of the Universal Christian Church. All clergy were declared free to use the Book of Common Prayer in public worship. In these terms of union, which the clergy of Qualified Chapels were asked to accept, it was also declared that such clergy must acknowledge the Bishop of their diocese as their spiritual governor under Christ and pay such canonical obedience as is usually paid by clergy of the Church, and promise faithfully to perform the duties of their charge,

---

[1] Skinner, *Annals*, pp. 334–350 and appendix containing Bishop Jolly's address; Grub, vol. 4, pp. 115–121; Walker, *Bishop Alexander Jolly*.

when collated, and study to advance the welfare of the people committed to them.[1]

A number of clergy of separated congregations accepted the conditions of union, and they with their congregations were welcomed into the Church. One of the leaders of such clergy was Dr. Daniel Sandford, who was later elected Bishop by the Edinburgh clergy and in due course consecrated at Dundee in 1806.[2] At this time, and since Dr. Drummond settled in Edinburgh in 1787, the see of Glasgow was joined to that of Edinburgh. Dr. Drummond, while continuing to be responsible for the oversight of the Glasgow diocese, resigned his charge of Edinburgh in order to facilitate the election of Bishop Sandford. When the former died three years later, Glasgow was once again united with Edinburgh and remained so till Dr. Russell was consecrated Bishop of Glasgow and Galloway in 1837.

General Synods and a Comprehensive Code of Canons

The Episcopal Synod met in Aberdeen in 1809 and agreed to six Canons, the main provisions of which were that the clergy of one diocese should take no directions from any Bishop or presbyter of another diocese; that the rubrics prefixed to the Communion Office should be strictly observed, and that no innovations should be permitted in the service without the Bishop's consent; and that the clergy have the right of appealing from the sentence of their own Bishop to the Primus and the other Bishops of the Province.[3] The need of a Canon calling attention to the observance of the rubrics is illustrated in a statement of Bishop Gleig: " I found that I could not officiate for some of my own clergy without either showing the people that he and I think differently of our forms of prayer, or taking a lesson from him before going into chapel."

[1] Skinner, *Annals*, p. 553.
[2] Ib., pp. 358–404, 479; *Remains of Bishop Sandford*, vol. 1, p. 48.
[3] Skinner, *Annals*, pp. 483–493; Grub, vol. 4, p. 126; Walker, *Bishop George Gleig*, pp. 268–277.

The first General Synod since the Revolution was held at Aberdeen. The reason for calling the Synod was that the Code of Canons required to be revised and brought up to date. It is significant that whereas the Episcopal Synod had issued the Canons of 1743 and the six Canons of 1809, the Synod which met in 1811 to revise the Canons was composed of all the Bishops, four Deans, and a clerical representative from each diocese. This assembly was declared to be a regular National Synod of the Episcopal Church in Scotland. Nevertheless, as the Primus explained in opening the Synod, the clergy had the privilege of discussing all matters of discipline and canonical regulations to be set before them, but they had no decisive vote. He then suggested that the clergy retire to a separate chamber and with their elected chairman discuss the business before them and submit the results of their deliberations through their chairman to the Bishops. The clergy accepted the privilege, elected James Walker, the Dean of Edinburgh, as their chairman or prolocutor, and retired to consider each Canon as proposed.

The result of these deliberations issued in the publication of the Code of Canons of 1811, based on the 1743 Code with emendations and additions. The new Canons were comprehensive in their scope, dealing with Ecclesiastical Synods, Ordinations, the Thirty-nine Articles, Institutions and the Right of Presentation, the Scottish Communion Office, the studies and qualifications of candidates for Holy Orders, the residence of clergy in their districts, the services of the Church on Sundays and weekdays, the prevention of irregularities in the conduct of services, the care of chapels, preparation for Holy Communion and provision of opportunities of communicating at least three times a year, conditional Baptism, visits of Bishops and administration of Confirmation, the Marriage Service, Visitation of the Sick, Burial of the Dead, and repelling from the Holy Communion of notorious offenders.

In the Canon on Ecclesiastical Synods, the Bishops showed their wisdom in admitting presbyters to a share in legislation by providing that every Synod to be called for the purpose of altering the Code of Canons shall consist of two chambers, of which the second shall be composed of the Deans and representatives of the clergy, one from each diocese where there are more than four presbyters, and that every Canon must have the approval of both chambers.

All ordinands, before ordination, were to be required to subscribe the Thirty-nine Articles, to abjure the doctrine that princes excommunicated by the Pope might be deposed, to acknowledge the royal supremacy, and to promise obedience to the Canons of the Church.

The right of presentation to a charge was declared to belong to those who provided for the pastor's support. Rules were laid down, for institution to a pastoral charge, which forbade any person taking upon himself the charge of a congregation before his deed of presentation was accepted by the Bishop.

While the Scottish Communion Office was commended " as the authorized service of the Episcopal Church in the administration of that sacrament ", permission was given to use the English Office in those congregations which had recently come under the jurisdiction of the Scottish Bishops. The Scottish Communion Office was to be used in all consecrations of Bishops, and every Bishop, when consecrated, was to give his full assent to it, " as being sound in itself, and of primary authority in Scotland ".[1]

In an appendix to the 1811 Code of Canons a recommendation of a proper clerical habit is added, declaring that it is not essential to the purity of public worship whether the clergyman, when reading prayers, be arrayed in a white or in a black vestment, yet " as the white vestment was the proper sacerdotal vestment of the Jewish priesthood, and likewise of the Christian priesthood

---

[1] Skinner, *Annals*, pp. 505–517; Walker, *Bishop George Gleig*, p. 278; MS. Register of College of Bishops, vol. 1, pp. 60–93; Canons, printed at Aberdeen, 1811; Grub, vol. 4, pp. 126–135.

throughout the Universal Church for at least fourteen hundred years, as it is the proper sacerdotal vestment in the United Church of England and Ireland, and as white seems to be a much more proper dress for the ministers of the Prince of Peace than black, the Synod recommends to the clergy of this Church to wear the surplice when publicly reading prayers or administering the sacraments ". Apparently the black gown alone was in common use throughout the Church. It will be noted that the picture of the Seabury Consecration suggests that the black gown was in general use by the Bishops.

A further revision of the Code of Canons was issued on the authority of the General Synod which met at Laurencekirk in 1828, under the title, " The Code of Canons of the Protestant Episcopal Church in Scotland." Most of the Canons were close copies of those enacted in 1811, but there were a few changes and additions. For example, it was enacted that the Primus was to hold office for life, unless he refused to consecrate a presbyter canonically elected to the Episcopate, whose election had been confirmed by the majority of the Bishops, and also that General and Diocesan Synods were to be held regularly, quinquennially and annually respectively.[1] During the following year, a Synod at Edinburgh decided that General Synods need not be called so frequently.

Loyalty to the King

George IV, who became King in 1820, visited Scotland two years later and took up his residence in the ancient palace of Holyrood. His Majesty received an enthusiastic welcome from all classes of his Scottish subjects and not least from Episcopalians. The six Scottish Bishops were received at Holyrood and testified their loyalty to their King in the name of the Church, in the form of an Address, in which they said: " So many years

---

[1] Canons, printed at Edinburgh, 1828; Grub, vol. 4, pp. 181–185; MS. Register of College of Bishops, vol. 2, pp. 14–41.

have passed away since Scotland was honoured by the presence of its sovereign, that, to behold your majesty in the palace of the long line of our ancient monarchs, your majesty's royal ancestors, is to us, as it must be to every true Scotsman, a matter of pride and exultation; and in this house, more especially, do we feel ourselves prompted by these emotions to declare that, within the wide compass of your majesty's dominions, are nowhere to be found hearts more loyal than those which beat in the breasts of the Scottish Episcopalians. The devoted attachment uniformly displayed by the members of our Church to him whom they have considered as their legitimate sovereign is so well known to your majesty, that it would be waste of time to repeat it here, and is, indeed, amply vouched by the lowly station which we, her Bishops, now hold in society." The King was well pleased with the address, and is said to have been particularly struck with the venerable appearance of Bishop Jolly.[1]

The Co-operation of the Laity

In the course of a visit paid to Scotland at this time, Dr. Hobart, Bishop of New York, impressed upon a number of churchmen the wisdom of encouraging laymen to co-operate in the fullest possible way in the practical administration of the Church.[2]

John Skinner,[3] elder son of the Primus, and for forty-five years rector of Forfar, became a warm supporter of the policy of admitting laymen to a share in the management of Church affairs. He advocated the presence of laymen in mixed conventions as well as in Diocesan Synods. In a circular letter which he addressed to the Bishops and clergy, he declared, " As things are now constituted, we have nothing to interest our laity, or

[1] MS. Register of College of Bishops, vol. 2, pp. 1–4; Walker, *Bishop Alexander Jolly* and *Bishop George Gleig*.
[2] Grub, vol. 4, pp. 175–177; Neale, *Life of Bishop Torry*, pp. 112–117.
[3] Author of *The Annals of the Episcopal Church in Scotland*.

excite their powerful co-operation. At present, they are left in entire ignorance of everything but the right or wrong discipline of their immediate pastor's duty.'' Though deprecating lay interference in purely spiritual matters, he urged that they be allowed a voice in all matters of temporal concern and in framing rules of lay discipline. He believed that the Church would gain immeasurably in matters that were purely secular by the co-operation of the laity, and by their advice and business experience.

Since the Revolution the management of the Church had been almost entirely in the hands of the Bishops, though the other clergy now had a share in the administration of the Province. However, there still lingered a fear of giving the other clergy and the laity a reasonable share of corporate responsibilities. Mr. Skinner, in his letter, stated that ever since the Synod of 1811 the Church as a corporate body had been in a state of total in-action, while every other denomination of Christians in Scotland had been assiduously busy in schemes of self-enlargement.[1]

It is undoubtedly a fact that the Church made less advance in the first half of the century than in the second, and that one of the powerful influences in its development in the last quarter of the century arose from the presence of lay representatives in the Church Council and its various Boards and Committees. However, Mr. Skinner's proposals were so far in advance of his time that many years passed ere the reforms he visualized came into service.

Rome and Paris

In the winter of 1817–1818, Dr. Walker, at that time Pantonian Professor of Theology and incumbent of St. Peter's, Edinburgh, during a visit to Rome instituted the now well-established custom of providing an Anglican service for British residents there.

About the same time, Dr. Matthew Luscombe was administering to British and American residents in Paris as a priest of the

---

[1] Grub, vol. 4, p. 176.

Church. He suggested that a Bishop be consecrated to exercise superintendence over clergy and congregations of the Anglican Church on the Continent, but the English Bishops would not move without the sanction of the Government, which the Prime Minister was unwilling to give. He then applied to the Scottish Bishops, and was, after some delay, consecrated Bishop at Stirling by the Primus and the Bishops of Edinburgh and Ross. Bishops Torry and Skinner protested against the consecration because they questioned the prudence of the proceeding. In the Deed of Consecration, the consecrating Bishops disclaimed all pretence of assigning diocesan jurisdiction to Bishop Luscombe, and declared, '' We do solemnly enjoin our right reverend brother not to disturb the peace of any Christian society established as the national Church in whatever country he may chance to sojourn, but to confine his ministrations to British subjects, and such other Christians as may profess to be of a Protestant Episcopal Church.'' [1] The consecration of Dr. Luscombe is chiefly noteworthy as a precedent which has been followed by the Church of England.

The State of the Church in 1838

It is convenient to attempt an estimate of the condition of the Church in 1838, for this year marked the beginning of new developments in terms of the Canons agreed to by the General Synod held at Edinburgh then, and particularly the setting up of the Church Society.

In the forty-six years which had passed since the repeal of the Penal Laws, many new congregations came to life, though the meeting-houses or churches were generally very poor and small. Sometimes small cottages would serve as churches, sometimes rented rooms in a town tenement, and in a few cases small church buildings erected on a chosen site. Clergy and

[1] MS. Register of College of Bishops, vol. 2, pp. 5–7; Neale, pp. 118–138; Blatch, *Life of Bishop Low*, pp. 96–126.

laypeople alike proved very ready to provide themselves with more adequate church buildings and parsonages, and several efforts were made with this end in view. The story of many congregations in Scotland recalls the struggles of the Church to re-establish itself on the Scottish soil, as, for example, in St. Andrews, where the congregation first met in leased premises, then in a beautiful church of limited size erected in this period, and later from 1860 in a handsome set of church buildings still in use. A mission from this congregation has developed in more recent years, and now possesses a beautiful stone church, church halls, and club-rooms.

In 1838 the Church was emerging from the " doldrums ", and here and there throughout Scotland congregations were busily engaged erecting necessary buildings or seeking to acquire leased premises, so that at this time the Church was represented in about one hundred congregations. The clergy suffered severe conditions of poverty. There was no adequate means of providing for their material needs. Generally they were left entirely to the generosity of their small and poor congregations, and consequently the stipends of most of them were merely nominal. More than a third of the congregations had an annual income of less than £80. It is astonishing that so many of the clergy were able to lead their people forward to the building of necessary buildings at a time when they themselves were suffering such poverty.

There was no adequate means of providing for the education of candidates for the sacred ministry, though it is of interest to recall that as early as 1810, a parishioner of Bishop Jolly, Miss Kathrein Panton, left a sum of money to erect and endow a " Seminary of Learning or Theological Institution for the education of young men, desirous to serve in the Sacred Ministry of the Scotch Episcopal Church ". The first Pantonian Professor of Theology was the Rev. James Walker, afterwards Bishop of Edinburgh, who probably lectured to three or four students in his own house year by year during the period 1824–1841. Already, therefore, the opportunity was being provided to prepare the clergy who would lead and guide the Church in the years to come.

There was little opportunity for Home Mission enterprise organized from the central councils of the Church, but Bishops in their dioceses and clergy and laypeople in their congregations were ever actively concerned to push forward into new centres as opportunities appeared. Thus within the early years of the nineteenth century the foundations were being laid for the development of the life of the Church.

9

THE REVIVAL OF THE CHURCH (1838–1900)

DURING the period between the Synod of Edinburgh in 1838 and the close of the nineteenth century the Church in Scotland extended its work and influence in a remarkable way.

The General Synod of 1838

The Synod which met in Edinburgh revised and added to the Code of Canons, dropping out the word " Protestant " in the title. The second Canon enacted that the Primus was to hold office only during the pleasure of his colleagues. The fourth Canon provided for the appointment of coadjutor Bishops, for whose appointment no canonical sanction had previously been given. The Scottish Office was to be used at the opening of General Synods as well as at the Consecration of Bishops. The use of the surplice, formerly recommended, was now enjoined. Formal canonical sanction was given for the formation of " The Scottish Episcopal Church Society " to provide a fund for aged and infirm clergymen or salaries for their assistants, and general aid for congregations struggling with pecuniary difficulties; to assist candidates for the ministry in completing their theological studies; to provide Episcopalian schoolmasters, books, and tracts for the poor; and to assist in the formation and enlargement of diocesan libraries.[1]

The Oxford Movement

We cannot trace the story of the revival of the Scottish Church without stumbling again and again upon evidence of the

[1] MS. Register of College of Bishops, vol. 2, pp. 67–97; Canons, printed at Edinburgh, 1838; Grub, vol. 4, pp. 191–195.

work of the Oxford Movement. It would be arbitrary, even if it were possible, to attempt to disentangle the work of the Oxford Movement from the developing life of the Church. In the revival of the Scottish Church many influences were at work, and amongst these influences a very high place must be found for those who found inspiration from the great movement which was already beginning to sweep across the Church of England. Many Scottish churchmen hailed the Oxford Movement with delight, precisely because its promoters were seeking to maintain principles for which the Episcopal Church in Scotland had contended through many decades in spite of much discouragement and organized opposition. Leaders of the Movement in England found encouragement in the example of Scottish churchmen, and a correspondence took place between some of them and the Scottish Bishops. An English clergyman acknowledged the comfort and support thus received, in the following words: " The clear calm note of Christian confidence and hope, which sounded from the Bishops of the Scottish Church, was like a voice from heaven, and we thanked God and took courage." A great-grandson of Bishop Rose of Edinburgh, at that time a rector in England, played an important part in the origin of the Movement, and perhaps Sir Walter Scott, himself a convert to the Church, had considerable influence in directing men's minds to the traditions of the Middle Ages, traditions which he enshrined in noble ideas and romantic pictures.

Though the traditional faith of the churchmen of the north could be pointed to as evidence of the Church's existence and continuity, the Penal Laws had so crippled the Church's life that Bishops and clergy alike were somewhat despondent and perplexed. The Oxford Movement brought encouragement to Scottish churchmen and inspired new visions and fresh zeal. We can trace its influence in the founding of Glenalmond Theological College and School for the training of a native ministry, in the building of churches at Jedburgh and Edinburgh (St. Columba's), in the founding of the Cathedral at Perth, and in the establishment of the College of the Holy Spirit at Cumbrae. New churches which were erected throughout Scotland expressed, in beauty of architecture and of worship, alike the revival of the Church and the influence of the Oxford Movement.[1]

The Church Society

The fortieth Canon enacted by the General Synod of 1838 provided for the setting up of the Church Society to provide for the poor and aged clergy, to assist candidates for the ministry, and to help forward the cause of education. Every congregation was expected to contribute an annual collection to the funds of the Society. Bishops as well as other clerical and lay supporters in England made donations to the Society to help the work of the Scottish Church. The need of such a Society is evident from the fact that many incumbents were receiving merely nominal stipends.

" Where is the man who can peruse the scattered hints of the sorrows and exiles of Episcopalians between 1748 and 1792 without at least some thrills of admiration for men who, having nailed their flag to the mast of principle, were determined to stand by their colours to the last, whether they waved in the sunshine of calm, or were rent in the gloom of the tempest? " This rhetorical question was asked by the Rev. R. Montgomery of Glasgow at the first anniversary meeting of the Society when he reminded churchmen that they were living in a milder atmosphere as " a tolerated and not a triumphant, a protesting not a prosperous church ", and then urged the need of providing schools and churches in many parts of Scotland.

It is thrilling to read in the annual reports of the Society how deeply concerned the clergy of the Church were to regard their work as a mission to the people of Scotland, though inevitably preoccupied with the necessity of providing a more adequate

[1] Perry, *The Oxford Movement in Scotland*.

minimum stipend for the poorest-paid clergy, and also to support by grants the promotion of new congregational centres whenever possible. One of the first results of the Society's work was the provision of a minimum stipend of £80 per annum.

Statistics were quoted at one of the early meetings of the Society as evidence that there were more than ten thousand Episcopalians in Glasgow destitute of the ministrations of the Church.[1] Yet, when the incumbent of Leith, the Rev. Michael Russell, was consecrated Bishop of the united diocese of Glasgow and Galloway in 1837, the number of worshipping churchpeople in the diocese was said to be so small that they could all be accommodated conveniently in a reasonably large drawing-room. Bishop Russell continued to minister to his congregation at Leith, making only occasional visits to his diocese.[2] Yet within a few years several churches, mission halls, and schools were established in the Glasgow diocese, and the work of building up what is now the largest diocese, in the number of its members, was begun.

It is significant that the Church's mission to the poor and destitute is invariably associated with the need of providing schools and teachers, and it is remarkable that in spite of the difficulties encountered, so much progress was made in this direction that within twenty years more than £10,000 had been contributed in grants in aid of schools, in addition to assistance in the provision of school buildings, and the number of schools had risen from ten to eighty-five.[3]

During the same period (1838–1858) the number of churches increased from seventy-three to 150, parsonages from fifteen to fifty-six, and clergy from seventy-eight to 163. In this revival the Church was well blessed in the leadership of Bishops who were concerned as pastors of their people to provide meeting-houses and appoint clergy when the opportunity appeared.

---

[1] Church Society Annual Reports.
[2] Walker's *Three Churchmen* gives an account of Bishop Russell and his writings.
[3] Church Society Report, 1859.

Frequently the only accommodation available was in rented premises, and the stipends provided were miserably inadequate. Nevertheless, there were not wanting devoted priests prepared to accept their responsibilities and to struggle with difficulties so that the work of the Church might go on.

Notable amongst the Bishops who led their clergy and people forward into vigorous missionary work is Bishop Alexander Penrose Forbes of Brechin. At the time of his consecration in 1847, Bishop Forbes was also incumbent of the Episcopal congregation in Dundee, which met in a meeting-house in Castle Street. Under his leadership plans were carried forward for the building of St. Paul's Church, now the Cathedral of the diocese, and four other churches were provided in the city of Dundee as part of his mission work.[1]

The Church Society made an important contribution to the development of the Church during the thirty-eight years of its active life, and the Rev. E. B. Ramsay, later Dean of Edinburgh, was enabled to serve the Church in a valuable way through his endeavours in connexion with it. William Ewart Gladstone was a keen supporter of the Society, and at one of its meetings he expressed gratification at the opportunity given to him to testify in public the deep interest which he took in the affairs of the Scottish Church, and declared his confidence in its revival.[2]

Removal of Legal Disabilities

A bill was introduced into Parliament by the Archbishop of Canterbury in 1840, and in due course passed both Houses and received the royal assent. Its intention was to remove some of the disabilities imposed on the Scottish Episcopal Church when the Repeal Act was passed in 1792. The new Act gave Scottish Bishops and priests the privilege of ministering for one or two Sundays in any church in England.

A more satisfactory bill was carried through Parliament in

[1] Perry, *Alexander Penrose Forbes*.   [2] Church Society Annual Reports.

1864 which removed the restrictions altogether, so that clergy in Scottish orders were placed on an equality with clergy of the Church of England and made eligible for any ecclesiastical office or benefice in the Church of England with the consent of the Bishop of the diocese.[1]

The Act of 1864, in removing the restrictions, also testified to the practical union of the Episcopal Church in Scotland and the Church of England. Leading ministers of the Scottish Presbyterian Established Church were not slow to note this aspect of the situation and to express their opposition. One such minister, Dr. Robert Lee, regarded the Act as conferring a peculiar privilege upon a rival Church.[2]

Regium Donum

In 1814 a number of influential friends of the Church succeeded in obtaining from the Government a grant of £1200 every second year, known as the Regium Donum. This grant was divided equally amongst the clergy of the Province. Forty-two years later, however, on the initiative of Mr. Gladstone, this grant was withdrawn because it tended to produce the false impression that Episcopacy in Scotland was quite well endowed. In its place a number of laity introduced a Regium Donum Compensation Fund as an endowment sufficient to yield at least the same amount in interest as was received in the government grant.[3]

The Representative Church Council

The development of the Church during the third quarter of the nineteenth century called for the provision of an organization based on a broader system of finance than that of the Church

---

[1] W. Stephen, vol. 2, pp. 607, 645–646.
[2] Lee, *Reform of the Church of Scotland*, c. 6, " Secession to the Episcopal Church and its Causes ".
[3] W. Stephen, vol. 2, p. 574.

Society and for the services of laymen in the whole field of administration. The Church Society was mainly a collecting agency, distributing its income to assist congregations in poor circumstances. In 1871, however, an important development of the work carried out by the Society was introduced by the inauguration of an Equal Dividend Scheme, into which congregations made their offerings, the incumbents of such congregations receiving in return an Equal Dividend supplementary to the local stipend. This Scheme was carried forward into the Representative Church Council when it was formed in 1876, at which time one hundred and forty-five congregations were on the Equal Dividend List, and the income was distributed in equal shares of £63, with three shares to each Bishop.

Membership of the Representative Church Council was to include all the orders of the clergy, lay officials, lay diocesan representatives, and a lay representative from every incumbency and mission. While taking over the work which had been done by the Church Society, the Representative Church Council was committed to developing the Church's activities in other directions. The Primus, the Bishop of Moray, who presided at the first annual meeting of the Church Council in 1877 in Glasgow, introduced the first report and said, " I think it may be well just to show how we have prospered, and where, perhaps, an opportunity may be offered to us to advance, for we cannot stand still, and advance we will." He described the object of the Clergy Sustentation Fund thus: " To give permanency to the progress which the Church has made by improving the means and strengthening the status of our clergy, and this not only by increasing their temporary incomes, but by providing, as it were, a permanent income equivalent to endowment, which may place them where they ought to be, in an entirely independent position."

It is clear from the first Report and also from the address of the Primus at the first annual meeting that one important concern of the Council was the extension of the Church, and, in particular, the promotion of missions. To this end a General Board of Home Missions was set up at that first meeting. It is noteworthy that the reason given for the encouragement and promotion of Home Mission work is " our true claim to be the ancient and historical Church of Scotland ". [1] Nine years after the inauguration of the Church Council, the Home Mission Association was formed to encourage churchpeople to pray, work, and give for the extension of the Church, and an offer was accepted from the Rev. C. Jubb to give his services, without salary or travelling expenses, as organizing Secretary for Home Missions.

A detailed statement was published with the Church Council Reports year by year showing the progress being made in Home Mission work. Most of the mission congregations met in rented premises and were making considerable efforts towards the provision of new buildings. It is a fascinating study to examine these annual statements, to follow from year to year the development of mission congregations from their rented premises, to " iron huts " or timber erections, and step by step to the erection of permanent churches, halls, and parsonages. In all this development, much was expected from the local congregations, but the Home Mission Board was also ready to help in the making of grants for maintaining curates or assisting building schemes.

During the twenty-five years of the Council's work before the close of the century considerable progress was made and twenty-five new congregations were added to the Clergy Fund Equal Dividend List, while many mission centres were brought into being. In 1899 there were one hundred and seventy incumbencies and some fifty or sixty missions at various stages of development. A beginning was made with the formation of a Capital Account for the Clergy Fund, and at the close of the century a total of £11,000 was accumulated.

[1] R.C.C. Report, 1877.

The scope of the Council's work extended to the cause of education, and in particular the provision and maintenance of Church Schools. In his address, to which reference has already been made, the Primus at the first meeting of the Council said, "I look upon education as one of the most important objects which this Council can take under its care. No Church can expect continuity if it neglects the education of its own children in its own faith." The Board of Education, with representative Boards in each diocese, was given the charge of supervising and planning a general system of religious instruction of all church children, and especially in the Church Schools.[1]

In spite of the many calls on its resources and interest, the Scottish Church did not hesitate to rise to the call of service in the work of the Church Overseas. In 1871 the Scottish Bishops received a communication from the Bishops of South Africa pointing to the need of missionary work in Kaffraria. The call was answered, and Dr. Callaway was consecrated Bishop in Edinburgh to supervise the work in Kaffraria. A short time later, at the instigation of the Primus, responsibility was accepted for the mission district of Chanda in India. And so the Board of Foreign Missions came into being to support the Church in Kaffraria and Chanda.[2]

The importance of providing for the training of candidates for the service of the sacred ministry was recognized for many years before the Representative Church Council came into being. It was noted above that Bishop Petrie, during the eighteenth century, at his own house at Folla provided theological courses for ordinands, of whom Alexander Jolly was one. Later Bishop Jolly continued this good work in his house at Fraserburgh, and in 1810 a parishioner there, Miss Panton, left a sum of money for the building and endowment of a theological seminary. The

---

[1] R.C.C. Annual Reports, 1876–1900.
[2] MS. Register of College of Bishops, vol. 4, pp. 17–25, 30; *Scottish Guardian*, 1871, p. 277, and 1873, p. 382.

first Pantonian Professor of Theology, the Rev. James Walker, was born in Fraserburgh and was probably a pupil of Bishop Jolly. When he became Bishop of Edinburgh he continued to teach theological students, probably in his own house. His successor as Bishop of Edinburgh, Charles H. Terrot, also continued his duties as Professor of Theology. Later, for some thirteen years, the college was centred at Glenalmond, but this arrangement did not prove satisfactory, and the Scottish Bishops agreed that a more convenient centre would be in Edinburgh. John Dowden brought the College to Edinburgh again in 1876, though for a time it had no fixed centre. A house in Rosebery Crescent was, however, rented in 1880, and twelve students came into residence. Ten years later the Representative Church Council purchased Coates Hall and provided a chapel, a library, and extra bedrooms, and, under Principal Keating, the College moved into the buildings which it still occupies.

Addressing the annual meeting of the Council in 1899, the Bishop of Moray said: "It is always difficult to gauge the progress of our Church from year to year in this land. It is only when we look back over some considerable period that we are able to see the extent to which God has been pleased to vouchsafe to her renewed prosperity and strength. We stand to-day in the closing year of another century, and the time seems fitting for a retrospect as well as for a glance at the possibilities in the future. At the beginning of this century the Church was just emerging from the gloom and depression which was the result partly of the long continued severity of the Penal Laws. Let us contrast her position then with that which she afterwards attained, and, thank God, occupies to-day."

The Bishop then presented two vividly contrasting pictures, one the dedication of a little cottage meeting-house in Keith at the beginning of the century, and the other the consecration of a Bishop in Edinburgh Cathedral at the close of the century. He then continued: "You know how in the period under review our churches have been multiplied; how in that very city of Edinburgh, where, at the beginning of the century there were but two, or at the most, three churches of our communion, there are now twenty-five churches and missions. In Dundee, where, in the memory of some still living, our services were held in an upper room in one of its principal streets, there are now twelve, and among them some noble churches and missions. The same cause for thankfulness may be found in Glasgow and other of our large towns.''

In speaking of Home Mission work, the good Bishop said: '' This is the Church's most precious offering to present before the feet of our Lord and Master. We may thank God for it, that year by year, this offering is brightening as she rises to the greatness of her opportunities. May we not hope and pray that in the beautiful little chapel attached to our Theological College in Edinburgh, one and another of the students may hear a voice say to him: ' Whom shall I send, and who will go for us ? ' and with lips purified by the living coal from off the altar, may make reply and say: ' Here am I, send me '.''

The Services of the Church

In the Aberdeen diocese, and generally in the north, the preference, at least amongst the clergy, was for the Scottish Communion Office. In the diocese of Edinburgh the preference was for the Communion Office of the Church of England. Throughout the nineteenth century, controversies continued over what office ought to be followed at a celebration of Holy Communion.

The Canons of 1838 required that General Synods were to be opened with a celebration of the Holy Communion according to the Scottish rite. Twenty years later, however, the General Synod of 1863 enacted that while the Scottish Office might be continued in all congregations whose practice it was to use that Office, in all new congregations the Communion Office of the

Book of Common Prayer of the Church of England was to be used. Further, it was declared that the Scottish Office might be dropped whenever the clergyman and a majority of the communicants of his congregation concurred in disusing it.[1]   In the revisions of the Code of Canons in 1875 and 1890, this position with regard to the use of the Communion Office was maintained.

Much controversy persisted over the use of the two Communion Offices, some vigorously commending the use of the Scottish Office and some as strenuously opposing it.   Bishop Ewing urged that one Communion Office should be regarded as authoritative for the whole of Scotland, and suggested that all parties in the Church would be united if the English Office were generally adopted.   " By the retention of the Scottish Office, we keep alive a confusion of tongues among us, make havoc of the Church, and run the risk, by uncharitably forgetting the weak, of destroying ' him with our meat for whom Christ died '." [2]

There are frequent references in letters and tracts of the nineteenth century to the need of mission services, with a clear missionary and evangelistic aim, and at the same time the setting up of missions which would provide such services.   St. John's Episcopal Chapel, in Glasgow, was set in a populous industrial district.   The incumbent, however, had been guilty of introducing such innovations as the intoning of prayers, the chanting of psalms, turning to the east when the creed was said, omitting the prayers before and after sermon, and chanting or intoning the responses after the commandments.   In his letter of criticism of the incumbent, the Bishop wrote: " The history of the last few years, and the special means which I have had of observing the effect upon the mind of an ever-growing and ever-craving taste for a more symbolical and imaginative ritual, than our

[1] MS. Register of College of Bishops, vol. 3, pp. 94–292.   The Rev. George Hay Forbes, Burntisland, raised an action in the Court of Session disputing the power of the Synod to alter the status of the Scottish Office, without success (*Scottish Guardian*, 1865, p. 198, and 1867, p. 232 ; Perry, *George Hay Forbes*).

[2] Ross, *Memoir of Bishop Ewing*, pp. 280–297.

system has practically sanctioned, has impressed me most deeply with the danger of such indulgence. I exhort those whom it is my duty to exhort to be content with the simple but decent ritual which has been usual in well-ordered Churches.''

Revisions of the Code of Canons

The development of the Church's life and work is reflected in the revisions made to the Code of Canons by the General Synods of 1859–1863, 1875–1876, and 1890.

The chief changes introduced in 1863 were to admit a lay representative from each congregation to vote in the election of a Bishop; to permit laymen, if invited by the Bishop, to address diocesan Synods; to sanction the appointment of lay readers and catechists; to admit curates and mission clergy of three years' standing in the diocese to membership of Synod, and to a vote in the election of a Bishop; to restrict clerical vestments to those in use at that time; and to remove the Scottish Communion Office from its position of primary authority as the authorized service of the Church and to adopt the English Book of Common Prayer as the service book for Scotland. Further changes in the Canons regulated the position of curates, and constituted the offices of diocesan chancellor, registrar, and auditor. The Canon in restraint of vestments appears to be a reaction against the ritualistic movement in England.

The changes made in the Canons by the General Synod of 1875–1876 reflect the growth of the Church and are mainly concerned with matters of administration. More explicit regulations were formulated for the setting up of incumbencies and the opening of new missions. The membership of the General Synod was enlarged by the admission of one representative for every ten, or fraction of ten, members of each Diocesan Synod. The chief business of this General Synod, however, was to give canonical sanction to the Representative Church Council, '' the organ of the Church in matters of finance only ''.

The General Synod of 1890 considered a proposal to revive the title and metropolitan powers of the primate, but the proposal was strongly opposed by the lower house and thrown out as unsuitable to the circumstances of the Church. A number of changes in nomenclature were agreed to: for example, the Primus was to be assigned the title of " Most Reverend ", the title " Rector " was substituted for " Incumbent ", " Provincial Synod " was substituted for " General Synod ", and a congregational lay representative for the election of a Bishop was to be called a " lay elector ". A new Canon was introduced on Cathedrals, and another was added regulating the formation and defining the status of mission congregations. The Canon dealing with the Representative Church Council was made more specific by the declaration that the Council " shall not deal with questions of doctrine or worship, nor with matters of discipline, save to give effect to Canonical Sentences of the Church ".[1]

The State of the Church in 1900

Episcopacy was slow to recover from the depressing effects of the long century of persecution and restrictions, but as the nineteenth century ran its course it was clear that the Church in Scotland was rising to quickened life. Cathedrals were being erected at Perth, Inverness, and Edinburgh. Magnificent churches were being erected in all the cities of Scotland and in many large towns, and congregations were springing to life in industrial areas and country towns, from the populous districts of Glasgow and Dundee to the country towns like Wick and Galashiels.

At the close of the nineteenth century, stately cathedrals, many fine church buildings, and nearly three hundred congregations though some were numerically small, testified to the astonishing expansion and development of the Church in the generations which had passed since the repeal of the Penal Laws.

[1] Canons of the Episcopal Church in Scotland, 1863, 1876, and 1890.

Within the Church itself a number of remarkable changes took place in the conduct of public worship. Early in the century, churches were very plain and without chancels. The only vestment worn by the clergy was the black gown. The services were without musical accompaniment. The psalms were always read. The Holy Communion was celebrated only three or four times a year. Yet, at the close of the century, it was customary to find surpliced choirs and musical services, with the accompaniment of finely-toned organs, and monthly or weekly celebrations of the Holy Communion, and in places a daily Eucharist.

It is undeniable that one of the outstanding features in the development of the Church in Scotland was its close approximation to the Church of England. This process was clearly marked at the Convocation of Laurencekirk, when it was agreed to accept the Thirty-nine Articles of Religion and when the movement of union with the Qualified Chapels was being mooted and advanced. Step by step, from the introduction of the surplice by the clergy to the general use of the Book of Common Prayer of the Church of England, the process went on. The final removal by Parliament in 1864 of the disqualification of Scottish clergy from officiating or holding a benefice in England drew the two Churches even more closely together.

The nineteenth century was clearly a period of remarkable expansion and development for the Scottish Church. At the time of disestablishment, the Episcopal Church offered little to the nation of either faith or worship which it did not already possess, except an Episcopal polity. By the close of the nineteenth century the Church had recovered its Catholic heritage. It adhered firmly to primitive truth, and it possessed an ordered pattern of liturgical worship, a constitutional Episcopacy, and a deepened sense of missionary responsibility.

The number of souls attached to the Church in 1900 was estimated at one hundred and sixteen thousand, of which total forty-six thousand were communicants. Thus the Church was numerically but a tiny minority in relation to the population of Scotland.[1] Many of the congregations possessed only temporary buildings, in the form either of iron or timber constructions, or of rented shops, rooms, or halls. Much planning and much sacrificial giving were necessary if more worthy buildings were to be provided for worship.

Churchmen in 1900 looked forward with hope to the development of the work which had prospered so well, and Bishops and other clergy showed themselves ready to turn their energies to the next stages in the Church's expansion. Amongst the laity, too, were a number of great-hearted and optimistic workers in the common task, as members both of the Representative Church Council, its Boards and Committees, and of the many congregations of the Province.

[1] R.C.C. Reports; *Scottish Guardian*; Mitchell, *Biographical Sketches of Scottish Church History*, " John Dowden ".

10

BISHOPS OF THE CHURCH (1792–1900) [1]

WHEN the Penal Laws were repealed in 1792, John Skinner was Bishop of Aberdeen, John Strachan was Bishop of Brechin, William Drummond was Bishop of Edinburgh, and Andrew MacFarlane was Bishop of Moray, Ross and Caithness with Argyll.

In this chapter, which will be divided into seven sections, we shall note the development of the Church in the seven dioceses with reference to the work and witness of the Bishops of this period.

The Diocese of Aberdeen

There were only four Bishops of Aberdeen in the one hundred and twenty years from 1786 to 1906, and they were John Skinner (1786–1816), William Skinner (1816–1857), Thomas Suther (1857–1883), and Arthur G. Douglas (1883–1906).

John Skinner was the second son of the Rev. John Skinner of Linshart and shared part of his father's imprisonment when he suffered under the penalties of the 1748 Act. He was educated at Marischal College, Aberdeen, and after ordination he was placed in charge of two country congregations in the Aberdeen diocese, and soon afterwards returned to the city of Aberdeen to minister to the Episcopal congregation which met in the meeting-house in Longacre. After four years as coadjutor Bishop to Bishop Kilgour, John Skinner succeeded him as Bishop of the diocese. He continued as incumbent of his Aberdeen church for many years, and led his people in their efforts to provide a more

[1] This chapter is based upon notes and articles in contemporary issues of the *Scottish Magazine*, the *Scottish Guardian*, the Church Society Reports, and the Representative Church Council Reports; with the help of the relevant Biographies included in the Bibliography, and the *Dictionary of National Biography*.

worthy church building in the Church of St. Andrew, erected in 1795, and now the Cathedral of the diocese. As Bishop he did much to encourage churchpeople throughout the diocese in their efforts to provide church buildings to replace the former meeting-houses. We have already noted the important part he took in the consecration of Samuel Seabury, the repeal of the Penal Laws, the union with the Qualified Chapels and in the first efforts towards a practical revision of the Code of Canons to regulate the affairs of the Church. He was an enthusiastic advocate of the use of the Scottish Communion Office and as Primus, though acting without constitutional authority, he required Patrick Torry and George Gleig, before their consecration as Bishops, to promise that they would do all in their power by personal example and by any other means open to them to encourage the use of the Scottish rite.

William Skinner, the second son of Bishop John Skinner, was educated at Marischal College, Aberdeen, and at Wadham College, Oxford, where he graduated in arts and divinity. He was ordained deacon and priest by the Bishop of Rochester, and served for a short time in the diocese of St. Asaph, before returning to Scotland as assistant and, in due course, successor to his father as incumbent of St. Andrew's Church in Aberdeen. On his father's death, he was elected by the Aberdeen clergy as Bishop of the diocese. He was assiduous and exemplary in the discharge of his episcopal duties, and did much for the welfare and consolidation of the Church. In 1832 he administered the sacrament of Confirmation to 462 persons in his diocese. With the approval of the Synod of Aberdeen, Bishop Skinner excommunicated Sir William Dunbar, the incumbent of St. Paul's Church in Aberdeen, for refusing to receive or administer the Sacrament according to the Scottish rite.

For over seventy years, John and William Skinner, father and son, occupied the see of Aberdeen and led their people through the days of deep depression, after the long and severe political persecution, to happier times of toleration when the Church was permitted to live its own life as a free and independent communion.

Thomas Suther was educated at Windsor College, Nova Scotia, and after ordination in Edinburgh served curacies there before becoming incumbent of St. George's Chapel in that city, and later incumbent of St. Andrew's Church in Aberdeen. He was elected Bishop of Aberdeen by the clergy of the diocese and duly consecrated. His diocese was enlarged to include Orkney. It was shortly after the opening of his episcopate that a charge of unsound teaching on the sacrament of the Holy Eucharist was made against the Rev. P. Cheyne, incumbent of St. John's, Aberdeen. The trial took place in the Diocesan Synod, and soon afterwards Bishop Suther gave his judgement suspending Mr. Cheyne from his office as presbyter of the Episcopal Church in Scotland. On an appeal to the Episcopal Synod, it was found that all the Bishops, except Bishop Forbes of Brechin, upheld the Bishop of Aberdeen. Four years later, however, after making explanations to the Bishops, Mr. Cheyne was restored to his full ecclesiastical status.

Arthur Douglas was a graduate in arts and divinity of Durham University, and had served as a priest in Kidderminster, Southwark, Scaldwell, and Shapwick before he was elected Bishop of Aberdeen. A centenary celebration of the Seabury consecration was held at Aberdeen at the beginning of the episcopate of Bishop Douglas, and was attended by eighteen Bishops and over two hundred other clergy. During his episcopate, Bishop Douglas confirmed nine thousand and fifty-seven persons, and the communicant membership of his diocese increased from five and a half thousand to six and a half thousand. He was a strenuous protector of poorer charges, particularly the smaller country charges, which were suffering the drift of population to the towns. New churches were erected at Fraserburgh, Aberdeen (St. James's), Bieldside, Folla Rule, Insch, Burravoe, and Braemar, while new mission work was initiated at Ballater, Braemar, and the dock area of Aberdeen. Many parsonages and a number of schools were also provided. It was largely as a result of his patient endeavours that the separated congregations of St. James and St. Paul in Aberdeen were reunited with the Church.

The Diocese of Argyll and the Isles

The persecution under the Penal Laws was particularly harsh in the Western Highlands so that the Church was almost completely destroyed. An account has survived of a priest of the Church, " John Connachar, of irreproachable character and of considerable attainments ", who was charged with a breach of the statutes in performing divine service on a number of occasions. He was found guilty and sentenced to perpetual banishment. It is remarkable that in spite of such severe treatment a number of clergy continued to minister to churchpeople in the Western Highlands, and Bishops like Robert Forbes and Arthur Petrie found it possible to visit their flocks.

In 1792 Bishop MacFarlane of Moray also superintended the diocese of Argyll. Indeed, we may regard the diocese of Argyll as united with Moray until the appointment of Alexander Ewing as Bishop of Argyll and the Isles in 1847. His successors were George Mackarness (1874–1883) and James R. A. Chinnery-Haldane (1883–1907).

Alexander Ewing was presbyter at Forres in Ross-shire when he was chosen to be Bishop of the scattered congregations in Argyll and the Isles. Bishop Low described him as a sincere Christian and a gentleman, " one who had not sought the Episcopal office merely to make a livelihood out of it, and gain honour at the same time, but who had private means of his own, which freed him from any such unworthy imputation, and which would enable him to maintain, with sufficient external dignity, the position he had been chosen to fill ". Writing of the part of his diocese around Glencoe and Ballachulish, Bishop Ewing said,

" The only remnant of the past here is the Church. The lairds of Appin are gone; the old holders of the lands and property are no more; but the Church remains, notwithstanding emigration, dispossession, and deaths, pretty much as before. Charles Stuart and his race are all extinct, but the creed of the nonjurors still holds its ground in the Strath of Appin, in Lochaber, and Glencoe."

Bishop Ewing could number only six congregations in his diocese in 1847, with a maximum number of 487 communicants, at Ballachulish, Fort William, Portnacroish, Dunoon, Rothesay, and Stornoway. Soon after his arrival he made the acquaintance of the people of Oban and arranged that services be held in a house, afterwards in the Caledonian Hotel, then for some years in an old masonic hall, and in 1863 the first stone of a church was laid. Congregations were also brought together and incumbents appointed at Lochgilphead and Campbeltown. In some ways one of the most interesting events of his episcopate was the founding of the church on the island of Cumbrae. The first step was the opening of St. Andrew's Chapel in 1848. Mr. George Boyle, afterwards the Earl of Glasgow, had in his head and in his heart a scheme and a desire to found in Cumbrae a church and college of priests, where the worship of God would be continually celebrated, and to which priests and others could retire for study, meditation, and prayer. The first step in the carrying out of this scheme was taken when the foundation stone of the church was laid in 1849. Three years later, the church and the south and the north college were in use. Unfortunately, as a result of a financial crash, the story of which does not concern us here, the scheme to endow the Collegiate Church at Cumbrae did not materialize, but as the Cathedral of the Isles it continues to serve many useful purposes, and not least as the church for the people of the island.

George Mackarness, Vicar of Ilam in Staffordshire and brother of the Bishop of Oxford, was elected Bishop of the diocese in succession to Bishop Ewing, and was consecrated in St. Mary's, Glasgow. During his short episcopate churches were built at Innellan, Inveraray, Glencreran, Glencoe, and Nether Lochaber, and the beginning of work on the islands of Skye and Mull was discussed. The Collegiate Church of the Holy Spirit at Cumbrae was constituted the Cathedral of the Isles.

He was succeeded by the Dean of the diocese, James Chinnery-Haldane. The new Bishop was a graduate in law of Cambridge University, having intended to follow in the footsteps of his father as a barrister. After short curacies in Salisbury and Edinburgh, he became incumbent of the new church at Nether Lochaber, and soon afterwards took over the pastoral oversight of the congregation at Ballachulish and the mission at Glencoe. He was elected unanimously, and during the years of his episcopate he proved himself to be a patient, kindly, and saintly pastoral Bishop. His great work was to build upon the foundations already laid and to encourage the congregations and church families in the villages of his scattered diocese. He provided a considerable endowment for several of the charges.

Diocese of Brechin

Five Bishops occupied the see of Brechin in the period under review, John Strachan (1788–1810), George Gleig (1810–1840), David Moir (1840–1847), Alexander Penrose Forbes (1847–1876), and Hugh W. Jermyn (1876–1904).

When Dr. Drummond was elected Bishop of Brechin in 1787, he stipulated that he should have a coadjutor. John Strachan, presbyter of the Episcopal congregation in Dundee, was chosen as coadjutor Bishop and, a year later when Dr. Drummond settled in Edinburgh, succeeded as Bishop of the diocese. With Bishops Skinner and Drummond, John Strachan went to London to petition the Government for relief from the Penal Laws. Several churches in the diocese maintained an almost unbroken tradition of loyalty to the Church during the years of persecution, notably the congregations in Dundee, Arbroath, Brechin, Drumlithie, Laurencekirk, Lochlee, Montrose, Muchalls, and Stonehaven.

George Gleig was educated at King's College, Aberdeen, and after ordination he settled at Pittenweem. After fourteen years there, he took charge of the congregation at Stirling. At that time there was no regular church at Stirling, but the congregation normally assembled in a room which formed part of an old turreted house. Three years after the repeal of the Penal Laws he led his people to occupy their first regular church building, " a plain structure, oblong in form, without a chancel ". He remained incumbent at Stirling for some years after he was consecrated Bishop of Brechin. On three occasions he was elected Bishop of Dunkeld, but the election in each case was rendered ineffectual by the Bishops. A distinguished scholar in mathematics and the moral and physical sciences, George Gleig was a contributor to the *Encyclopædia Britannica* and edited the last six volumes of the third edition.

As Bishop of Brechin, he urged upon his clergy the importance of conformity in the conduct of public worship. He complained, " I am afraid that some of us deviate widely from the words of the Liturgy; that we destroy the effect of its venerable antiquity, by modernizing some of its expressions; that we interpolate the Liturgy, and other parts of the public service, with petitions, or clauses of petitions, composed by ourselves." Bishop Gleig expressed a preference for the Scottish Communion Office, describing it as " a more faithful copy of the ancient offices, especially in the Greek Church; and were it in my power without disturbing the peace of the Church, I would introduce it, not only into every chapel in the diocese, but into every church and chapel in the British Empire ". He took an important part in the preparation of the Canons of 1811, and showed himself a wise legislator.

Though not outstanding as an administrator, Gleig proved

himself to be a wise and patient leader. The separated congregations were gradually coming under the jurisdiction of the Scottish Bishops, but in some places the union was as yet only mechanical. The situation was particularly difficult when two congregations, one Scottish Episcopal and the other a former Qualified Chapel, existed side by side. A situation of this type existed at Stonehaven, and a spirit of hostility developed. In due course, however, the two congregations became united, and the priest of the Episcopal Church, on the death of the priest of the Qualified Chapel, continued to minister to both congregations in Stonehaven till they were happily brought together.

A delightful picture of Bishop Gleig was given by Bishop Torry. "He always wore a short cassock, with knee-breeches and buckles and silk stockings, and when he had occasion to go out in the town to pay a visit it was a pleasant picture to see the trim old gentleman, pacing along the street, with his shovel hat, and gold-headed staff."

During the last ten years of his episcopate Bishop Gleig was unfit, because of age and infirmity, to superintend his diocese. On several occasions he sought the help of a coadjutor. In 1835, he wrote, "I completed my eighty-first year yesterday, and have not been able these five years to go into bed or come out of it, and far less to go up and down stairs, without help. The consequence is that I have not visited my diocese these six years, nor has the sacred ordinance of confirmation during that long period been regularly administered in it." The increasing infirmities of their Bishop decided the clergy of Brechin to apply to the Episcopal College for a mandate to elect a coadjutor.

David Moir, incumbent at Brechin for thirty-six years, was elected coadjutor to Bishop Gleig and consecrated Bishop in Edinburgh in 1837. On the death of Dr. Gleig three years later, he succeeded as Bishop of Brechin. Like most of the Bishops of the period, David Moir was also incumbent of a congregation during his episcopate, for he remained at Brechin until his death in 1847. For a short time during his episcopate, Alexander Forbes, destined to be his successor in the Bishopric, served as incumbent of the church at Stonehaven.

The " amiable Bishop Moir ", as he has been described, found himself faced with many administrative problems, largely as the result of the inability of his predecessor to attend to the needs of the diocese. One of the matters which had been neglected was provision for the pastoral care of Episcopalian congregations in the fishing-villages of the diocese. Bishop Moir sought to remedy this state of affairs, but he was not able to do more than encourage the congregation at Catterline and to provide them with a clergyman and to secure assistance for the building of a small church.

Alexander Penrose Forbes was Vicar of St. Saviour's, Leeds, when he was elected to the see of Brechin in 1847. A true son of the Scottish Church, and yet one who was deeply influenced by the Oxford Movement, Bishop Forbes has been justly called " The Scottish Pusey ". Though he was Bishop of Brechin for twenty-eight years, he was only in his fifty-eighth year when he died. During these years he was also incumbent of St. Paul's, Dundee, continuing his work as a faithful pastor amongst the people to whom he ministered at first in the meeting-house in Castle Street and after 1853 in the fine church, now the Cathedral of the diocese. Deeply concerned about mission work amongst the poor in Dundee, he inspired assistant clergy to go into several populous districts of the city and seek to win round them congregations of people ready and willing to accept the ministrations of the Church, and as a result of their efforts four firmly established missions developed and noble and worthy church buildings were erected. The important work done by Bishop Forbes as a pastor in Dundee and district is still clearly demonstrated by the strength of the Church in that city even to this day.

Almost from the day of his consecration, Bishop Forbes was involved in controversy. In 1857 he delivered a charge to his clergy on the Holy Eucharist, in which he laid chief stress upon the real presence of Christ in the Sacrament, the lawfulness of the worship of Christ sacramentally present in the elements, and the Eucharist as a sacrifice as well as a communion.

Some months later, in spite of the objections of Bishop Forbes, the Episcopal Synod resolved to send a pastoral letter to the Church, to be communicated by each of the Bishops to their Diocesan Synods, on the subject of the charge and condemning its teaching. Bishop Trower of Glasgow showed himself clearly opposed to the teaching of Bishop Forbes and urged his clergy to renounce such false teaching. Judicial proceedings were adopted by the Episcopal Synod, and the finding announced was that in certain respects the teaching of Bishop Forbes was not sanctioned by the Articles and Formularies of the Church, and was to some extent inconsistent with them. At the same time it was noted that since the Bishop only asked toleration for his opinions and did not claim for them the authority of the Church, or any right to enforce them on those subject to his jurisdiction, the Court limited its sentence to a declaration of censure and admonition.

In addition to his many activities as a faithful and hard-working pastoral Bishop, Bishop Forbes found opportunity to give the Church the benefit of his learning through his studies in theology, history, hagiology, and devotional commentaries.

Hugh Jermyn was a graduate in arts of Cambridge, and after serving a curacy in Kensington he became Rector at Forres and soon afterwards Synod Clerk of the diocese of Moray, and later Dean. After only six years' service in Scotland he became Archdeacon of St. Christopher's, West Indies, and, some years later, Bishop of Colombo. On the death of Bishop Forbes, Hugh Jermyn was elected unanimously and became Bishop of Brechin in 1876. '' The new Bishop conscientiously endeavoured first of all to enter into the spirit which animated the work of Bishop Forbes, and then to carry on that work with an appreciative love of the methods." During his twenty-seven years as Bishop of the diocese, four new incumbencies were established, thirteen new churches were built, and several missions, schools and halls were built or enlarged. The membership of the diocese increased from twelve thousand to twenty thousand, and the number of communicants from four thousand to seven thousand. He urged upon his clergy the necessity of providing at least a weekly celebration of the Holy Communion, and the number of celebrations of Holy Communion increased from twelve hundred in 1876 to four thousand in 1902.

Diocese of Edinburgh

The Bishops of Edinburgh during the period under review were William Drummond (1787–1806), Daniel Sandford (1806–1830), James Walker (1830–1841), Charles H. Terrot (1841–1872), Henry Cotterill (1872–1886), and John Dowden (1886–1910).

William Abernethy Drummond, a presbyter in Edinburgh, was elected and consecrated Bishop of Brechin, but he made the stipulation that he should have a coadjutor, presumably because he intended to remain in Edinburgh. Resigning Brechin in favour of his coadjutor, Dr. Drummond devoted his attentions to the Church in the Edinburgh diocese. At this time most of the Episcopal congregations in Edinburgh were served by clergy who had " qualified " and were therefore outside the jurisdiction of the Scottish Bishops. Dr. Drummond assisted in the efforts to gain the repeal of the Penal Laws and urged forward the proposal to unite the Qualified Chapels and the Episcopal congregations of the meeting-houses. To facilitate an effective union, he resigned the see of Edinburgh (though retaining oversight of Glasgow for three more years) in the hope that a priest of one of the former Qualified Chapels might become Bishop.

Daniel Sandford, of St. John's Qualified Chapel, was elected by the clergy of the diocese and consecrated Bishop in Dundee.

Bishop Sandford proved himself eminently suited to the difficult task of healing the breach between the two sections of the Episcopal Church. He was the first Englishman promoted to a Scottish Bishopric. During his episcopate most of the separated congregations in Edinburgh came under the jurisdiction of the Scottish Bishops, and notably St. George's Chapel, the first Episcopal Church built in the new town of Edinburgh, in which Sir Walter Scott, a faithful convert to the Church, worshipped with his family at this time.

James Walker, who was educated at Marischal College, Aberdeen, and at the University of Cambridge, was born in Fraserburgh, where he spent his early years under the pastoral influence of the saintly Bishop Jolly. After his ordination as deacon and priest he spent some years as tutor and chaplain to an Edinburgh family, with whom he travelled abroad. On his return to Scotland he became incumbent of St. Peter's Chapel and later the first Pantonian Professor of Theology. He succeeded to the Bishopric of Edinburgh in 1830, and continued to provide instruction in theology to ordinands seeking admission to the ranks of the sacred ministry. Some years before his election to the Episcopate, James Walker had been attacked by two of the English clergy of the diocese who were popular evangelistic preachers but who disliked the more distinctive principles of Episcopacy. James Walker, like the majority of the Scottish Episcopal clergy, clung to the teaching and traditions of the Caroline school of theology as represented by Andrewes, Laud, Cosin, and the later Non-Juring divines. A number of clergy from many parts of Scotland appealed to the Bishops to take action against those guilty of making unfounded statements about the teaching of their Church, and especially for slandering Dr. Walker. No action was taken by the Bishops, and the controversy died out.

Dr. Walker was an outstanding scholar, with an exceptional influence in the Church. He was sub-editor of and contributor to the third edition of the *Encyclopædia Britannica*, his special interests being philosophy and metaphysical inquiry.

Charles Hughes Terrot, a graduate in arts with honours in mathematics of Cambridge, was incumbent of St. Peter's, Edinburgh, and Dean of the diocese when he was elected Bishop in succession to James Walker. He also succeeded him as Pantonian Professor of Theology. He was a capable scholar both as theologian and mathematician, and edited the Greek text of the Epistle to the Romans. During his episcopate a number of churches were erected and opened for worship, notably the new Church of St. Peter, in which, since he had served the congregation for sixteen years as priest, he was particularly interested. All Saints' Church was also founded at this time.

An interesting experiment was made by the Bishop in appointing a Diocesan Missionary whose duty was to seek out poor people and others who were outside the Church and endeavour to link them up with the life of the congregation in the district where they lived. Thus the Missionary, though he conducted evening services in various hired halls, was not himself in charge of any congregation. An extract from his report in 1848 reads, "The design of the Home Mission has been, not to form of these neglected families a new and separate congregation, but to gather them into other congregations through the medium of my evening service. And, in order to effect this, we trust that the vestry of each church will be ready to grant a few free sittings even in the new town, for those of our poor who live nearest to them."

Henry Cotterill, Bishop of Grahamstown, was elected by the clergy and lay electors of the diocese to be coadjutor to Bishop Terrot and to succeed him on his death. The episcopate of Bishop Cotterill marks an important stage in the development of the Church in the Edinburgh diocese. The extension of the Church in new congregations which was noticeable during the episcopate of his predecessor continued, and amongst the new churches erected pride of place must be given to the Cathedral Church of St. Mary, the foundation stone of which was laid in 1874, and which was consecrated five years later. The building of this magnificent church was made possible by the generous benefaction of the Misses Walker.

A spirit of healthy enterprise prevailed in the seventies of the last century, and with it came a gradual widening of the powers of the laity in Church affairs, as illustrated in the formation of the Representative Church Council.

John Dowden, a priest of the Church of Ireland and a graduate of Trinity College, Dublin, was introduced into Scotland when he was appointed Pantonian Professor of Theology by the College of Bishops. On arriving at Glenalmond he found to his disappointment that his class was to consist of one solitary student. After some years, Dowden left Glenalmond for Edinburgh and strenuously resisted any attempts to oblige him to return. He said on one occasion, " The College may return to Glenalmond, but the Pantonian Professor remains here." For some years he gave instructions to students in various places in Edinburgh until a suitable place was secured in Rosebery Crescent, and later Coates Hall was purchased for the College. These years of teaching, with the opportunity provided him for study, gave John Dowden the chance of extending his interests in the field of Liturgiology and Church History, and in particular Scottish Church History.

As Bishop of Edinburgh he bore his share in the notable work of Church expansion and consolidation. The membership of the Scottish Church in 1870 was about sixty thousand, but at the time of Bishop Dowden's death in 1910 it had increased to about one hundred and twenty thousand. In the same period the number of churches had increased from about two hundred to about four hundred, and the number of clergy from about two hundred to about three hundred and thirty.

It is worthy of record that Canon Liddon, of St. Paul's, London, was elected Bishop of Edinburgh by the clergy and lay electors in

1886. In his letter declining to accept the appointment, he said, "There is another consideration on which I have in former times insisted with others, and which I could hardly set aside in my own case without inconsistency. In order to bring the true claims of the Church in Scotland before the mind of the Scottish people, with reasonable hope of success, it is important that her rulers and chief ministers should be Scotsmen. With Englishmen for Bishops, she will always, I fear, appear a foreign system in the eyes of a patriotism so naturally sensitive as that of the Scotch, and her worship and action will be described—as I often regret to hear it described in Scotland—as that of the ' English ' Church. I have not a drop of Scottish blood in my veins, so far as I know."

Diocese of Glasgow and Galloway

The dioceses of Glasgow and Galloway were united in 1837, and during the remaining years of the century the following Bishops occupied the united diocese: Michael Russell (1837–1848), Walter John Trower (1848–1859), William S. Wilson (1859–1888), and William T. Harrison (1888–1904).

The Bishops of Edinburgh generally exercised superintendence over the congregations in Glasgow and Galloway, but when Michael Russell, incumbent of Leith, added to his duties the Episcopate of Glasgow and Galloway, there were only three or four congregations in the south-west of Scotland. St. Mary's Church was erected in 1825, representing the interests of those churchmen who worshipped in various meeting-houses in Glasgow during the eighteenth century. The only other Glasgow congregation met in the English Qualified Chapel which was built in 1750, and which later joined the Scottish Episcopal Church as St. Andrew's-by-the-Green. The congregations at Dumfries and Ayr record a continuity of ministrations with the days of the Penal Laws, and only four years before the consecration of Michael Russell the Church of the Holy Trinity,

Paisley, was built. In spite of the fact that Bishop Russell made only occasional visits to his diocese, a number of new congregations came into being, for example at Hamilton, Helensburgh, and Girvan.

Walter John Trower was Rector of Wiston, Sussex, when he was elected, by eight votes to seven, Bishop of Glasgow and Galloway. After ten years' occupancy of the see, during half of which he was non-resident, he resigned and returned to England. Four years later he was appointed Bishop of Gibraltar. Bishop Trower was the first Englishman appointed to a Scottish Bishopric who had not previously ministered in Scotland. During his years of residence in the diocese he was also incumbent of St. Mary's Church. He did not understand the traditions of the Church in Scotland, and vigorously condemned and opposed every movement which seemed to him in line with the ritualistic developments of the Oxford Movement. He made himself prominent in opposition to the Eucharistic teaching of Bishop Forbes of Brechin.

William S. Wilson, Dean of the diocese and incumbent at Ayr, was elected Bishop and consecrated in St. Paul's, Edinburgh. Mr. Wilson was incumbent at Ayr for twenty-seven years before he became Bishop, and after his consecration he remained at Ayr for a further twenty-five years. During his episcopate a large number of churches were opened and many missions were founded. The present Church of St. Mary, now the Cathedral of the diocese, and the Church of St. Ninian, the first Episcopal church to be erected in Glasgow south of the River Clyde, were built at this time, in addition to churches at Ardrossan, Dalbeattie, and other towns.

William T. Harrison was Vicar of St. James's, Bury St. Edmunds, when he was chosen Bishop of Glasgow. His episcopate is specially notable for the remarkable expansion of the Church in the south-west; thirty new missions were established, twenty-nine churches and halls were built, and five missions were raised to the rank of incumbencies. Though Bishop Harrison inspired the movement of establishing mission centres in many areas within the city of Glasgow and in towns throughout the diocese, yet the task of consolidating this work and developing these centres involved many years of patient and devoted service on the part of many priests. The early years of the twentieth century were years of much activity in the erection of more worthy churches to replace the corrugated-iron structures which generally served as the mission centres in the days of Bishop Harrison. It is astonishing how optimistic and audaciously courageous clergy and churchpeople were in this period of expansion.

Diocese of Moray, Ross, and Caithness

The Bishops of the period under review were Andrew Mac-Farlane (Bishop of Ross and Argyll, 1787–1819), Alexander Jolly (Bishop of Moray, 1789–1838), David Low (Bishop of Ross and Argyll from 1819, and after 1838 of Moray also, till 1851; Argyll was separated in 1847), Robert Eden (1851–1886), and James B. K. Kelly (1886–1904).

Andrew MacFarlane was in charge of the congregation at Inverness before and after his consecration to the Episcopate. Dr. Johnson, who visited Inverness only three years before Andrew MacFarlane took charge of the church there, said, " There is an English chapel, but meanly built, where on Sunday we saw a very decent congregation."

Bishop MacFarlane's tombstone epitaph gives a brief account of his life: " The union of great vigor and power of mind, with corresponding bodily exertion, rendered him eminently qualified, for the Episcopal charge of the United Diocese of Ross and Argyle, over which he presided, with unwearied labour and dis-tinguished usefulness, for the long period of thirty-two years. During the last ten years of his life he solemnly consecrated for public worship six chapels in his own diocese, of the erection of which, as well as of the chapel in this place [Inverness], he was the chief promoter.'' Bishop MacFarlane resigned his charge of the diocese of Moray in 1798 in favour of Alexander Jolly, though he continued to superintend Ross and Argyll till his death in 1819. The clergy of Ross and Argyll unanimously elected David Low to succeed him.

Alexander Jolly was educated at Marischal College, Aberdeen, and after ordination was placed in charge of the congregation at Turriff, though later appointed to Fraserburgh, where he continued to minister to the faithful till the end of his life. In 1796 he was consecrated coadjutor to Bishop MacFarlane, but two years later the four presbyters of the diocese of Moray chose him as their Bishop, the Bishops having decided to disjoin Moray from Ross and Argyll.

Bishop Jolly observed the strictest discipline of time and food so that he might give every available hour to his studies and prayers. His daily readings included selections from the Hebrew *Torah*, the Greek New Testament, and the Apostolic Fathers. Dean Stanley of Westminster called him, '' A choice specimen of the old Episcopalian clergy.'' Dean Hook of Chichester referred to him as '' The venerable primitive and apostolic Bishop of Moray.'' He took an active part in persuading the clergy to accept the Thirty-nine Articles of Religion, and at the convocation of the clergy held at Laurencekirk in 1804 he referred to the Anglican Reformers and the Caroline Divines, who were primitive and Catholic in their teaching, as having cordially subscribed the Articles. The convocation unanimously accepted the Articles and thus paved the way for union with the Qualified Chapels.

During the visit of George IV to the Scottish Capital, the Bishops of the Episcopal Church were received by His Majesty, who is said to have been specially struck with the venerable appearance of Bishop Jolly. Indeed, the other Bishops seem to have been greatly perplexed about the wig of their brother prelate. The

Primus wrote to Bishop Torry, on the subject of Bishop Jolly's wig, that the Bishop of Edinburgh " seems absolutely nervous, alleging that the King will not be able to stand the sight of it, and assuring Dr. Russell that it would convulse the whole court ".

When Dr. Hobart, Bishop of New York, visited Aberdeen in 1824 and met Bishop Jolly he was so impressed that afterwards he described him as one of the most apostolic and primitive men he ever saw. By his great learning and saintly life, Alexander Jolly brought considerable prestige to the Church he loved so well and so greatly adorned.

David Low was educated at Marischal College, Aberdeen, and, after his ordination, was appointed to the charge of Pittenweem in Fife in 1789, where he remained until his death in 1855. During his incumbency, he led the congregation from their meeting-house in the High Street of that town to their new church and secured for them the ancient priory as a parsonage. On the death of Bishop MacFarlane he was unanimously elected Bishop of Ross and Argyll, and on the death of Bishop Jolly the diocese of Moray was added to his charge. In 1846 he resigned Argyll and the Isles and gave £8,000 towards the endowment of that diocese, to which Bishop Ewing was appointed.

Robert Eden, a graduate of Oxford in arts and divinity, was Rector of Leigh in Essex when he was elected Bishop of the small group of congregations in the united diocese of Moray and Ross, there being only some seven or eight congregations. During the thirty-five years of his episcopate a remarkable expansion took place. The congregation at Nairn was resuscitated and that of Aberlour formed, but perhaps the most outstanding achievement was the erection of St. Andrew's Cathedral, a church of considerable dignity and beauty, the foundation stone of which was laid by the Archbishop of Canterbury. The Cathedral was placed in Inverness, where Bishop Eden took up his residence, and thus a centre of operations was

I

established within the diocese. His predecessor had resided throughout his episcopate at Pittenweem, nearly 150 miles from Inverness. Bishop Eden was himself Provost of the Cathedral till his health declined, when his coadjutor succeeded him in that office.

James Butler Knill Kelly was a graduate of Cambridge. After a short period as curate at Abingdon, he became Vicar of Kirkmichael in the diocese of Sodor and Man, and then assistant to the Bishop of Newfoundland. Later he was chosen Suffragan Bishop of Croydon and, after a time, returned to Newfoundland as Bishop of the diocese. He returned to England on account of failing health and acted as Assistant Bishop of London, and then Commissary to the Bishop of Salisbury. He was welcomed to Scotland as coadjutor to Bishop Eden, whom he succeeded as Bishop of Moray, Ross, and Caithness.

For twenty years, first as coadjutor and later as Bishop of the diocese, Bishop Kelly laboured for the building up of the Church in the north of Scotland. Several new congregations were formed, and a number of churches were erected. Indeed, the number of congregations increased during his episcopate from fifteen to twenty-seven, though most of the new congregations have continued as missions or chapels-of-ease.

Diocese of St. Andrews, Dunkeld, and Dunblane

The Bishops of the period are Jonathan Watson (1792–1809), Patrick Torry (1809–1853), Charles Wordsworth (1853–1893), and George H. Wilkinson (1893–1908).

Jonathan Watson, when he was elected Bishop of Dunkeld, was presbyter at Laurencekirk, where he remained until his death.

Patrick Torry was presbyter at Peterhead when he was chosen to succeed Bishop Watson, and he also remained in his charge for nearly thirty years after his consecration, though Peterhead was certainly as far removed from his diocese of Dunkeld as

Bishop Low's charge at Pittenweem was removed from his diocese of Ross.

Bishop Torry caused a storm of opposition when he issued a service book called *The Book of Common Prayer, according to the use of the Church of Scotland*. The Episcopal Synod issued a statement that the book had no synodical or canonical authority and addressed a letter to the English Archbishops and Bishops to assure them that "neither the College of Bishops, nor the Church at large, was answerable for its publication". The first cathedral built in Britain since the erection of St. Paul's, London, was begun in Perth during Bishop Torry's episcopate. Only a small portion of the cathedral was opened and consecrated in 1850, but from the beginning it was clear that the purpose of the noble scheme was to provide a worthy setting for the higher ideal of liturgical worship to which attention was being drawn by the Oxford Movement. It is worthy of note that there were very few churchpeople in Perth when the cathedral was begun, and there were many voices raised in criticism of the apparent folly of planning such a magnificent church where there were so few church members. Yet, year by year, the congregation at the cathedral increased, and when in 1890 the nave was opened it was clear that the Cathedral Church of St. Ninian in Perth had become fully established in the life of the community.

Several congregations were established in the diocese (which was united with St. Andrews in 1842) during Bishop Torry's super-intendence, for example at Burntisland, Kirkcaldy, and Dunkeld.

Charles Wordsworth was warden of Trinity College, Glen-almond, when he was appointed Bishop of the diocese. During the forty years of his episcopate, many fine church buildings were erected in the diocese and a number of new congregations were established. The nave of St. Ninian's Cathedral at Perth was erected, a magnificent church was built in St. Andrews, and churches were opened in Leven, Bridge of Allan, Callander, and in several other towns.

In season and out of season, Bishop Wordsworth urged the importance of ecclesiastical union. In diocesan Synods, on public platforms, in letters to the newspapers, in books and tracts, and in correspondence he constantly called attention to the need of finding some basis for reunion between Presbyterians and Episcopalians to form one strong national Church. His scheme of reunion, however, was as unpopular with Presbyterians as it was with Episcopalians in Scotland.

George H. Wilkinson, who had resigned the see of Truro because of failing health, was unanimously elected Bishop of the diocese and duly enthroned in St. Ninian's Cathedral. Bishop Wilkinson after ordination had served a curacy at Kensington and had then been incumbent at Seaham Harbour and at Westminster (St. Peter's, Gt. Windmill Street, and later St. Peter's, Eaton Square). During the fourteen years of his episcopate in Scotland he took a leading part in the proposals for church reunion and assisted in the forming of the Christian Unity Association. He frequently addressed meetings of clergy and ministers of other denominations on the question of reunion of the churches. In the diocese he did his utmost to make the Cathedral at Perth the centre of diocesan activity, and towards this end he was the prime mover in raising funds for the erection of the Chapter House, Cloister, and Vestries. New churches were erected at Aberfoyle, Kirriemuir, Aberfeldy, and Burntisland, new mission work was begun in twenty places, and eighteen mission buildings provided. The membership of the diocese increased from six thousand to ten thousand, and the number of communicants from three thousand to nearly five thousand.

Bishop Wilkinson died in the Board Room of the Representative Church Council offices in Edinburgh after making a speech on a number of church matters. In the course of this speech he said, " I say unhesitatingly that, wherever you go, through the whole of the Anglican Communion, at least so far as I have had the opportunity of watching its work in different parts of the world, I believe you will find nowhere a body of men working more loyally with their Bishops, more heartily and unitedly with the clergy, and devoting more fully the best of their strength to help the work of the Church which is so dear to them.'' Thus Bishop Wilkinson paid his tribute to the great succession of laymen who have been invaluable guides and workers in the administration of the Church in Scotland.

11

CONSOLIDATION AND EXTENSION (1900–1950) [1]

THE history of the Episcopal Church in Scotland since the opening of the twentieth century illustrates the strength and vitality of the Church, which, in addition to consolidating what had been accomplished in the rapid growth of the closing decades of the previous century, formed a number of new congregations. The first two decades of the century continued the process of expansion so clearly developing in the later years of the nineteenth century, so that the membership of the Church, which was estimated at about sixty thousand in 1870 and about one hundred and sixteen thousand in 1900, had risen to one hundred and forty-seven thousand in 1921.

But alas, in spite of the fact that a number of new congregations were established in new housing areas and many church buildings were erected, there has been a serious decline in membership in the last twenty-five years, so that in 1950 the membership is shown to be only one hundred and eight thousand, or eight thousand less than at the beginning of the century.

The number of communicants rose rapidly from nine thousand in 1876 to forty-six thousand in 1900, and to nearly sixty thousand in 1921, but since then there has been a serious decrease of nearly four thousand. All the dioceses, except Moray, show decreases in the number of communicants at the present time compared with their communicant membership in 1921, Aberdeen and Edinburgh dioceses showing decreases of about one thousand each, while Glasgow, Brechin, and St. Andrews each show decreases

---

[1] For the writing of this chapter I have collected a great deal of detailed information from the Representative Church Council Reports, the Year Books, the *Scottish Guardian*, and the *Scottish Chronicle*.

of more than five hundred. At the present time much concern is being expressed at this serious state of affairs, and many causes, excuses, and explanations are being offered.

In this chapter, while not forgetting the statistical returns, from which the above extracts are quoted, we shall note the progress which the Church has made in the work of consolidation and extension.

Incumbencies and Independent Missions

The stipends of the clergy were generally quite insufficient for their needs before the First World War, but it was clear at the end of the war that a serious situation was facing the clergy because of the increasing cost of living. In these circumstances, a thorough overhaul of the Clergy Fund scheme was planned on the principle that every communicant of the Church ought to contribute to this central fund to assist the stipends of all the clergy, according to their needs. An organizer, John E. Macrae, later Dean of Brechin, was appointed to draw attention to the situation in all the congregations of the Province and also to appeal for generous donations towards the Capital Fund to provide a substantial annual income in the form of interest for the maintenance of the clergy. A large capital sum was contributed, and the annual income of the Clergy Fund was increased both by the interest on capital and from increased contributions. It was possible to plan a scheme whereby, in addition to a fixed equal dividend which was paid to all rectors and priests-in-charge of independent missions, the poorer clergy were given augmentation or supplementary grants to raise their stipends to a minimum figure fixed by the Church Council at its annual meeting each year. As a result of years of persistent effort it has been possible to provide the highest ever minimum stipend of £365 and a house or house allowance for 1950 to every rector or priest-in-charge in the Province.

The number of incumbencies and independent missions has

increased by about fifty to a total of about two hundred and fifty in 1950, partly as a result of the reorganization of the Clergy Fund in the 1920s when several missions were given the status of independent missions so that their clergy might share in the revised scheme, and partly by the adoption into the scheme of mission congregations which had become so well established as to be able to contribute most of the stipends of their priests locally.

Home Missions

The forming of new congregations has continued throughout the period under review. Since the First World War, three schemes have been promoted for the building of mission churches in the new housing areas which have been growing up throughout Scotland and chiefly around the large cities.

The first scheme, "The Million Shilling Scheme", was launched to provide funds for the buildings of six new hall-churches in new housing areas around Glasgow in the 1920s. These new missions were opened in Clarkston, Kings Park, Mosspark, Rutherglen, Knightswood, and Riddrie. Of these missions only two have become incumbencies, and the others are still mainly dependent on Home Mission funds for the stipends of the clergy in charge.

The second scheme, "The Home Mission Appeal", was launched to raise at least £30,000 for the erection of mission church buildings on various sites throughout Scotland, and the Rev. Canon Herbert Hall, at present Bishop of Aberdeen, was commissioned to organize the appeal. As a result of this appeal, more than £30,000 was contributed and new missions were established and church or hall buildings provided, or assistance in grants given, at Possilpark, Shettleston, and Hillington, in the city of Glasgow; at Stenhouse and Niddrie Mains in the city of Edinburgh; at Seaton and Hilton in the city of Aberdeen; at Mid-Craigie in the city of Dundee; at the village of Kemnay in Aberdeenshire; and at the mining town of Lochgelly in Fife

The missions established at Stenhouse and Hillington are now incumbencies, and much patient missionary work is being done in nearly all these centres.

The third scheme, " The Home Mission Crusade ", which was launched in 1944, had a double aim, first to raise the annual income of the Home Mission Fund from about £3,000 per annum to about £9,000 for the purpose of providing stipends for clergy who would engage in development and missionary work in connexion with existing charges or missions, or would pioneer in the establishing of new contacts whether as itinerant priests or as mission priests in new housing schemes. The second part of the scheme was to raise, in about ten years, at least £100,000 for the erection of churches or halls. The Rev. W. N. Gordon Boxer was commissioned to proclaim the message of the Crusade to every congregation of the Church.

As a result of the Crusade, which is still going on, hall-churches have been erected on several new sites in large housing areas, as at Sighthill and Moredun Park in the city of Edinburgh, and Pollok in the city of Glasgow; sites have been secured in several other districts, notably in East Kilbride, the new town being built in Lanarkshire; and grants have been given to assist the building of new churches at Clarkston and Springburn in the city of Glasgow, and halls at Lochee and Downfield in the city of Dundee, and at Comely Bank and Pilton in the city of Edinburgh. The above list does not exhaust the achievements of these recent years, for many congregations have been able to provide themselves with necessary additional buildings, notably parsonages, by local efforts.

For many years the stipends of curates and of priests in charge of missions were most inadequate, and varied greatly throughout the Province. Some improvement was effected when a new scale of Home Mission grants was adopted by the Representative Church Council in 1949. Mission priests are to receive the equivalent of the minimum stipend paid to rectors of incumbencies, while the stipends of assistant curates are arranged according to a scale rising from a minimum of £250 for a deacon to a maximum of £325.

The Church in Scotland is at the beginning of a great adventure in Home Mission development, if the necessary financial support is given. The Primus writes: " We have indeed good cause to thank God for the response that has so far been made to the appeal of our Home Mission Crusade by so many generous hearts; but we have a long way to go yet before we can confidently hope to reach even our immediate objectives. And beyond those there lies a vast field of possibilities yet to be explored, and further great tasks to be attempted." [1]

At the same time, there appears to be a tragic readiness on the part of many of the mission congregations to rest content with general subsidies in the form of grants, and to make no real effort to assist themselves, or even to justify their existence as missions by being centres of missionary endeavour, for many of these missions have really become simply " chapels of ease ". There are many who would maintain, in the words of a mission priest of 1895, " that the efficient consolidation of a few strong missions is, in our large towns, more conducive to the credit and spiritual efficiency of our Church than the starved existence of a larger number of weak ones ". There are more than a hundred mission congregations in Scotland at the present time, and of these over sixty have a communicant membership of less than one hundred persons.

The Home Mission task of the Church in Scotland is much more than the provision and maintenance of mission churches. It is, in short, the big task of the evangelization of the thousands of people in Scotland who are out of touch with the Christian Church; in that great number, there are thousands who were at one time practising churchpeople or who look to the Episcopal Church as to their own Church. The large influx of

[1] *Home Mission Crusade: Aims and Achievements* (1950), p. 3.

English families into Scotland, already considerable before the Second World War but even more marked during and since the war, and the fact that many of these families claim a nominal connexion with the Church of England, demand from the Episcopal Church in Scotland real and genuine efforts of evangeism in all the churches, whether cathedrals, incumbencies, or missions. It is clear that if the Church is to fulfil its claim to be the ancient and historical Church of Scotland, it must recognize its responsibility to the churchless thousands in the nation and do all it can to win them into living fellowship in the Church of Christ.

Building of Churches, Halls, and Parsonages

A considerable part of the achievements of the present century has been the erection of church buildings. At the opening of the century many congregations met in rented premises or iron buildings, and were without parsonage houses. Notable progress has been made in the provision of more worthy church buildings, generally of stone, some of which are buildings of great beauty. Church halls for the increasing social and recreational activities of the congregations, and houses for the clergy, have also been provided in many districts.

In most cases, though help has generally been given in the form of grants from the Walker Trust or other central funds, the carrying out of these building schemes has been the work of the local congregations. One of the most impressive and beautiful churches in Glasgow, St. Margaret's, Newlands, belongs to a congregation which was formed at the beginning of the century in a rented shop. Some years later, a hall was erected to serve as church and hall. Then, stage by stage, the present church was erected, and the church tower added as a memorial to the priest, Canon E. J. Petrie, who as the first Rector gave twenty-five years' service to the congregation and was mainly instrumental in carrying forward the scheme for the building of this worthy church. Another of the finest churches in the Province, though not yet completed, St. Bride's, Glasgow, replaces a corrugated-iron hut which served the congregation at the beginning of the century.

Though much has been done, much more remains to be done. Many church buildings are incomplete, and a number of congregations are seriously hampered in their activities by inadequate church halls. Far too many of our church sites are in side streets, and sometimes in out-of-the-way places. Where possible, there is need of a really bold policy of finding more convenient sites for some of the churches. Two examples of this policy illustrate the wisdom of making this experiment in many other instances. The missions at Shettleston and Possilpark had little chance of development until better sites were secured and more worthy church buildings erected. In both missions there has been a remarkable resurgence of congregational life.

The Theological College

The prayer expressed by the Bishop of Moray in 1899, " that in the beautiful little chapel attached to our Theological College in Edinburgh, one and another of the students may hear a voice say to him, ' Whom shall I send, and who will go for us ? ' and with lips purified by the living coal from off the altar, may make reply and say, ' Here am I, send me ' ", that prayer has been clearly answered in the period under review, for many of the students of the College have gone from its precincts to the missionary tasks in the parishes, consecrated in body, mind and spirit, dedicating themselves to the building up of the Church. Nearly half of the clergy on the active list are former students of the College.

The College has done a great work for the Scottish Church, and this is mainly due to the succession of able Principals who in their years of service inspired visions of pastoral and missionary service to successive generations of students. Canon Keating was Principal at the beginning of the century. He was succeeded by Canon Maclean, later Bishop of Moray, Ross and Caithness, and Primus; Canon Mitchell, later Bishop of Aberdeen; Canon Perry, later Dean of Edinburgh; Canon Brasnett, Canon Gillett, and Canon Lempriere.

The buildings of the College have been enlarged since the beginning of the century by the addition of the Principal's House, additional rooms, an enlarged chapel, and a large house, commonly called Forbes House because it houses the library of George Hay Forbes. Bishop Jolly's library is also preserved in Forbes House.

Overseas Missions

In addition to the many claims made upon churchpeople in Scotland for the maintenance and extension of work in the Province, nearly every congregation contributes annually to the special responsibilities of the Church in the diocese of St. John's, Kaffraria, and in the Chanda Mission, Central Provinces, India. Total grants to Kaffraria and Chanda amounted to over £11,000 in 1950. Far more important than the annual grants which have been made since the 1870s has been the succession of faithful missionaries who have gone from the Province to work in these mission fields overseas.

Education

There are thirty-five Church Day Schools throughout Scotland and about five thousand pupils attached to them. Only a little over a third of the teachers, however, are communicants of the Church.

In addition to providing grants for Sunday School work, the Education Fund of the Church has a large Central Fund, with a balance of nearly £17,000 in 1950, for the purpose of maintenance, improvement and extension of school buildings, and the provision of new schools. It is declared that Church Schools should be supported only in those places where they can be maintained in efficiency, and can contribute directly to the religious teaching of our own people or aid the missionary efforts of the clergy.

Social Service

The Social Service Board is the youngest Board in the Church. It did not come into being till after the First World War. It is, therefore, remarkable that the Church's work and interest in matters concerning social service has become so wide as it is to-day. Rescue work, with the provision of moral welfare workers and the support of several Rescue Homes, work amongst fisher folk in Scottish ports, youth welfare work, Eventide Homes, these are all supported by grants distributed by the Social Service Board.

The Dunderdale Trust

The generous bequest of Mr. C. H. Dunderdale in 1936, by which an annual income of more than £16,000 is distributed for the benefit of the Church, has greatly assisted the work of the Church in all the fields of interest to which reference has been made: the stipends of the clergy, the development of Home Mission work, the training of ordinands, the work of the Church Overseas, the cause of Education, and the various forms of Social Service to which the Church is committed. In addition, this generous bequest assists the funds which provide pensions for aged and infirm clergy and for widows and orphans of the clergy, and the funds for the endowment of Bishoprics and the building of churches and parsonages.

The Code of Canons

At the beginning of the century, the Code of Canons of 1890 was the subject of much discussion in the Diocesan Synods and elsewhere, with a view to a further revision, especially in the matter of giving a recognized position to the laity in the legislative work of the Church. Effect was given to this desire when a special Episcopal Synod and the Provincial Synod agreed in 1905 to add to the 1890 Canons an enactment constituting the Consultative Council on Church Legislation. The new Council was to consist of the Bishops, five clerical and five lay members elected by the Bishops, representatives of the clergy from each diocese in the proportion of one to every ten or fraction of ten clergy in the diocese, and an equal number of representative laity to be elected by the lay members of the Diocesan Councils. The Consultative Council was formed to focus the opinions of both clergy and laity on matters proposed or thought suitable for legislation in the Provincial Synod. During the next four years, the Council met from time to time and made a thorough revision of the Code of Canons, which was submitted to the Episcopal Synod for consideration by the Provincial Synod. In due course, the Provincial Synod of 1911 enacted the revised Code of Canons.

Election of Bishops. The right of nomination in the election of Bishops was extended to Lay Electors, and the voting was no longer required to be in separate chambers. If no election was made within three months of the date of the Mandate, power was given to the Electors, by a majority of each order, to delegate the election to the Episcopal Synod. If no election was made within six months of the date of the Mandate, the right of election was to lapse for that turn to the Episcopal Synod. Each Bishop was required to intimate to the Primus within twenty-one days whether he assented to the election or was dissatisfied with the suitability of the person elected. Female as well as male communicants were given the right to take part in the election of congregational Lay Electors.

Rectors absenting themselves from their cures without making provision for the supply of Sunday services and without giving a satisfactory explanation to the Bishop were made liable to be deprived of their incumbencies.

Services. The Scottish Liturgy, according to the text adopted by the Episcopal Synod in 1910, was authorized for celebrations of the Holy Communion throughout the Church. Congregations which had been using an earlier text were allowed to continue to do so.

The services of the Book of Common Prayer were authorized for all the services to which they were applicable, and a number of additions to and deviations from such services were declared to be permissible.

The normal standard was declared to be that the Holy Communion should be celebrated in all congregations every Sunday where reasonably practicable. Further, it was declared to be the duty of every Bishop, Priest, and Deacon to say the daily offices privately or publicly when he finds it practicable.

Clergy and congregations were given power to introduce a change in the use of the authorized Offices for Holy Communion, or to establish the use of both Offices.

Marriage. Clergy were forbidden to solemnize the marriage of anyone who had had a previous marriage dissolved *quoad civilia* by a civil Court, so long as the other spouse in the marriage so dissolved remained alive. The solemnization of marriage was forbidden to parties within the forbidden degrees, and the Table of Kindred and Affinity was re-enacted.

Congregational Districts. Districts were to be assigned to cures of souls, and every rector or priest-in-charge was required to keep a roll of the communicants of his congregation.

A number of new or revised Canons were enacted: on the subject of vestures of the clergy, and ornaments of the church; conferring the right to vote in Diocesan Synod on all duly licensed presbyters who had officiated in the Scottish Church for at least two years; and concerning accusations and appeals and procedure to be adopted in disputes.

The Revised Code of 1929

Soon after the First World War it was felt that the Code of Canons needed further revision, and after several years of deliberations the Provincial Synod passed, confirmed, and enacted the Code of Canons of 1929, which is at present in force, though discussions are now proceeding with the intention of revising and adding to the 1929 Code.

The changes introduced in 1929 are numerous, but many of them are concerned with the introduction of the Scottish Book of Common Prayer and will be referred to under that heading. Other changes of importance include the following:

Reunion. A significant addition to the Canons is that which provides the College of Bishops with authority, in view of some project of reunion, to invite representatives of other communions to give addresses in a church or churches in the Province, with the consent of the Bishop of the diocese and the rector or priest-in-charge of the church.

Ministry of Women. A new Canon declares that " The Order of Deaconesses is recognised by the Scottish Church ". The Episcopal Synod is given authority to approve the form and manner of making Deaconesses, but the following details are required: prayer by the Bishop and the laying on of hands, a formula giving authority to execute the Office of a Deaconess in the Church of God, and the delivery of the New Testament by the Bishop to each candidate.

Provision is made for Deaconesses, and other women in communion with the Scottish Church, to conduct, and to give addresses at, services in church other than and distinct from the canonical services, such services being intended for women and children.

Vesture. The Canon on vesture, which was adopted without change from the 1911 Code, states: " In the performance of the public services of the Church it shall suffice that Priests and Deacons be vested in surplices." The wearing of a stole or scarf, and of a university or college hood, is permitted, but the only mention of " other vestures " occurs in the requirement that because of " sundry inconveniences " which often arise from sudden changes in local uses, reference must be made to the Bishop, who is empowered to forbid or modify the change.

Missions. An additional Canon reflects the development of a number of churches, mainly in new housing districts, which were technically dependent missions. It was thought prudent to attach these missions to the Cathedral, and to place them under the control of the Bishop, who appoints the curates-in-charge.

The Scottish Book of Common Prayer, 1929

Dean Perry, in *The Scottish Prayer Book*, writes as follows of the 1929 Book: "It is catholic first and foremost, and Scottish and modern only in a subordinate sense. Yet, the Scottish Prayer Book has its own national history, especially in its liturgy which can be traced back through the Non-Jurors of the eighteenth century to the ill-fated Scottish Prayer Book of 1637. To the jibe that the Church in Scotland is no more than a mission from the Church of England a churchman now has a conclusive answer in the Scottish Book of Common Prayer."

The new Book, while following closely forms which are familiar to all who know the Book of Common Prayer of the Church of England, is a modern revision, with a number of additions and some re-arrangement. Additions were made to the Collects, Epistles, and Gospels; the Lectionary was revised, and Sunday Lessons at Mattins and Evensong were arranged in a three years' course; the reading of the Psalter was planned so that the Psalms for each Sunday might suit the general message of that particular Sunday in the Church's Year; Mattins and Evensong were revised slightly; an alternative form of prayers was provided for Evensong, to be said after the Third Collect; a form of Compline was added; the Litany was revised, and two Shorter Litanies added; additional Prayers and Thanksgivings with a Bidding Prayer were also provided; and a number of alterations and additions were made in the occasional offices. The Service of Holy Communion, as in the English Book, was adopted without any major revisions, but the Scottish Liturgy was thoroughly revised. Dean Perry in comparing the Scottish Liturgy with the English Communion Office wrote of " the immense superiority of the Scottish Liturgy in richness of thought, in beauty of structure, in order of sequence, and in dignity of expression ". The Consecration, the distinctive feature of the Scottish Liturgy, begins with the *Sursum Corda* as a call to thanksgiving and leads on to the *Sanctus* and *Benedictus.* The opening words of the Prayer carry forward this note of thanksgiving and praise, "All glory and thanksgiving be to thee, Almighty God, our Heavenly Father, for that thou of thy tender mercy didst give thine only Son Jesus Christ to suffer death upon the cross for our redemption." Then follows the narrative of the Institution of the Sacrament, and in logical sequence, the Oblation, " Wherefore, O Lord, we do celebrate and make here before thy divine Majesty, with these thy holy gifts which we now offer unto thee, the memorial thy Son hath commanded us to make." Next comes the Invocation of the Holy Spirit " upon us and upon these thy gifts and creatures of bread and wine, that being blessed and hallowed by his life-giving power, they may become the Body and Blood of thy most dearly beloved Son, to the end that all who receive the same may be sanctified both in body and soul ".

In his book, *The Scottish Liturgy*, Dr. Perry writes, " When the great time comes for a reunion that will give to Scotland one Church, at once Catholic and National, the Scottish Liturgy may play an important part in shaping the worship of the Scottish people at the Sacrament of unity."

The Scottish Book of Common Prayer is now in general use in the Province, though in many congregations the Scottish Liturgy is seldom used. The way in which the two long prayers, the Consecration Prayer and the Prayer for the Church, follow one another in unbroken sequence is a serious blemish in the opinion of many, precisely because, from the worshipper's point of view, the recital of these long prayers is conducive to wandering thoughts. For this reason there is a marked preference in many congregations for the Communion Office of the 1662 Book.[1]

In the foregoing pages, I have not attempted to describe in detail the controversy over the use of the Scottish Communion Office during the nineteenth century. The opposition was so strong, and the criticism so bitter, that many English and Irish churchmen formed " The United Church of England and Ireland " where they might use the service of Holy Communion in the Book of Common Prayer of the Church of England, and none other. There were many sympathizers in England. The Bishop of Worcester wrote in 1849: " In my opinion it was an omission in the Act of 1792 not to have required from the Episcopal Church of Scotland the adoption of our Liturgy. Till such adoption has taken place, it is impossible to consider the Episcopal Church of Scotland as in full communion with the Church of England." The secession described above was short lived, and only slight traces of it remain.

It is regrettable that the Scottish Communion Office was for a time deprived of its rightful place in the Church. Canon XXIX of the 1863 Code states that the English Book of Common Prayer shall be the Service Book of the Church. The Canons of 1911 did something to bring about a restoration of the Scottish Liturgy, in no small measure a result of the patient and scholarly work of Bishop John Dowden. The Canons of 1929 declare

[1] The Scottish Prayer Book, 1929; Perry, *Scottish Prayer Book* and *Scottish Liturgy*; Don, *Scottish Book of Common Prayer*; Gordon Donaldson, *Prayer Book* (1549–1949).

that the authorized Service Books of the Church are "The Scottish Book of Common Prayer approved by the Provincial Synod of 1929, and the Book commonly called the Book of Common Prayer of the Church of England ".

It would be tedious to follow out the provisions made in the 1929 Code of Canons for the adoption, in the several congregations of the Church, of the Scottish Liturgy or the English Communion Office, both of which are printed in the Scottish Book of Common Prayer. This happy conclusion to a controversy which divided the Church a century before has been achieved without any significant manifestations of partisanship. There is nothing in the present life of the Church which is comparable to the bitter opposition to the Scottish Liturgy in the 1840s. Some churches use the English Liturgy, and that alone. Some use the Scottish at one service and the English at another. Some use the Scottish Liturgy at every celebration of the Holy Communion.[1]

---

[1] A full account of the controversy inspired by " The United Church of England and Ireland " is given in the report of the debate in the House of Lords published, together with several partisan statements, under the title *Episcopacy in Scotland* (1849).

12

CHANGE AND READJUSTMENT (1950–1974)

THESE years are often described as " years of rapid change".
There can hardly be a period in the history of man which cannot
be so described, yet the changes in the twentieth century have
required of all Churches a readiness to adapt to changing circumstances and a willingness to meet the cost of such adaptation to a
degree which has few parallels. The period between 1920 and
1939 showed the vigilance and skill of church people in meeting
the needs of the times because there was a will to do so. Thus
the better provision of stipends for the clergy, the missionary
work and the buildings erected in the new housing areas, the
encouragement of vocations, and much else grew out of a deeply
felt concern to minister to the people of Scotland and to share
with them the good news of the Gospel as it had come to be
understood and expressed in the traditions of the Church.

The growth in church membership which marked the first
quarter of the century continued into the second quarter,
although there were already signs in the 1940s of a decline in the
number of members and communicants. Statistics of membership are notoriously misleading and particularly when there are
doubts as to the basis on which they are computed, or the effect
of " quota assessments " on returns from congregations. Early
in the century it was the generally accepted tradition to include
within the estimated membership every person who could be
described, however vaguely, as a baptised adherent. In more
recent years the tendency has been to give minimum figures.
Nevertheless there is no doubt of the sharp decrease in the
number of children brought for Baptism each year, and of the
decreased number of Sunday School children. The membership

of the Episcopal Church today is about 80,000, a decrease of 28,000 as compared with 1950, and 36,000 less than in 1900.

It ought to be easier to assess the number of communicants but here also there must be similar qualifications. There has been a serious decline in the number presented for Confirmation year by year. The present total of 46,000 communicant members is a decrease of 10,000 as compared with 1950, but is more or less as in 1900.

When the first edition of this book was published certain observations were made about the state of the church. These included criticism of its complex administration which bewilders many congregations and their clergy, of mission congregations which had become chapels of ease, and of clergy who make considerable changes and then leave their charges without being prepared to stay and build up the life of their congregations, and of clergy from England who make little or no effort to understand the traditions and heritage of the church. These past twenty-five years have underlined the force of these criticisms. At the same time there appears to be a more general willingness on the part of most lay people to accept changes, and a greater understanding on the part of most of the clergy. The Episcopal Church in Scotland has a considerable vitality, and in these years of change and readjustment has shown a fair amount of adaptability to changing situations.

Congregations

A great deal of change and readjustment has taken place in the congregations and much of it wise and forward looking. A number of small missions which reflected the social segregation of former years have been closed, and while there is some loss there is also considerable gain in such a change. The grouping or linking of small congregations and a more economic use of clerical manpower were inevitable as part of the process of readjustment. There still remains the far more important work of caring for people and maintaining a pastoral role of service to them. It cannot be said with confidence that in all instances there has been such a care. More often the changes made have been related simply to financial considerations, and have been governed by accountancy. There has been a considerable loss to the church in small communities where it is evident that congregations have become so small when regular pastoral care has ceased that in due course the church has virtually ceased to have any presence in these towns and villages.

The history of the Episcopal Church in Scotland through the years from the Revolution to the end of the nineteenth century is not so much the story of Bishops and Councils or Synods, but of the loyalty and devotion of the congregations, priests and their people. The twentieth century does not differ from the preceding ones in this. Congregational histories tell their own story. It may be that the account will begin with a meeting-house gathering, or regular services in rented premises, and in due course the building of a small chapel, the enlargement of it, or the erection and furnishing of a fine church. The story is not about these things but about the priests and people who achieved these as part of the way they came to express their religious convictions and their proclamation of the Gospel and devotion to their Lord. One of the best of these congregational histories is that of St. John's, Dumfries, written by Miss Jean S. Maxwell. There are many such accounts.

Recently formed congregations are adding their contributions to the faith and the worship of the church within their communities. The pioneering spirit of priests and people in the new towns of East Kilbride, Cumbernauld, Glenrothes, Livingston and Irvine adds to the record. It would be a mistake, however, to imagine that only in such centres can be seen the missionary work of the church and its continuing witness.

It would be to misunderstand the history and work of the church to assess its life in terms of the Representative Church

Council or the Provincial Synod, or the pronouncements of bishops. Boards and committees, councils, conferences and synods have their places in the life of the Church. They have an important function to enable the congregations of the Church to do their work, and they assist the congregations to see beyond their own boundaries to the needs elsewhere at home and overseas. Bishop J. R. H. Moorman in *A History of the Church in England* commented thus on the past twenty-five years: " The post-war age has been, therefore, the age of consultation, of conference and dialogue; and a feeling has grown up that every problem can be satisfactorily solved so long as enough people spend enough time talking about it, and that, if clergymen can be enticed away from their draughty vicarages to spend a few days in a centrally heated conference house, then the Kingdom of God has undoubtedly been brought a little nearer." Much the same might be said of these last twenty-five years in the Episcopal Church in Scotland.

Fewer Congregations and Fewer Priests

There are now 390 congregations, 70 fewer than twenty-five years ago, and they are served by 265 priests, 50 fewer. Many of these congregations are small mission charges or country incumbencies; one hundred and fifty have less than one hundred communicants.

The stipends of the clergy have fallen below that of the general level in the Church of England, and far below the minimum paid to ministers of the Church of Scotland. Increased capital, and increased income from it, has made it possible to maintain a level of stipend which took account of the rise in the cost of living. Increased costs for the maintenance and repair of buildings as well as for heating and lighting make it inevitable that economies are being forced upon the church. At the same time many congregations have shown a willingness to meet the challenge of the situation and have exhibited by their giving the measure of their response.

Home Mission Work

Change and readjustment mark the developing and enabling role of Home Mission support. New churches have been built in the new towns of East Kilbride, Cumbernauld, Glenrothes, and Livingston, and elsewhere in Scotland as in Aberdeen, at Mastrick; Glasgow, at Kings Park; Dumfries, at Lochside; Edinburgh, at Colinton Mains; and in the diocese of Moray at Poolewe and Balmacara. The purchase or the building of parsonages and church halls has gone on year by year, generally by the giving or fund-raising of the congregations themselves, but with some help from grants from central funds.

Ecumenical co-operation in Livingston New Town involves a team of ministers from the Church of Scotland, Congregational Union, Methodist and Episcopal Churches, in association with Roman Catholic Clergy. One of the churches in the group was built by the Episcopal Church and is designed to be used by all the churches in the ecumenical team. In a similar way other churches in the group are being shared.

Irvine New Town is expected to be the most populous area in Ayrshire. For some years a small congregation of Episcopalians was cared for by the rector of Troon and thus a foundation was laid. The congregation now meets in one of the Parish Churches in the town for a Parish Communion each Sunday morning, and ties of friendship have grown with the host congregation. This is an experiment in co-operation and sharing which may issue in the erection of a shared church, or a closer association with one of the existing churches.

Theological Training

The Theological College in Edinburgh has been reduced in size, part of the former buildings now having been taken over as offices for the Representative Church Council. The smaller college seems more than sufficient to house Scottish ordinands, a number of other Anglican ordinands, and guests. A closer link with the University of Edinburgh has been formed, following on the decision that all Anglican ordinands at the college should normally study for a theological degree of the University.

A new activity, which has already begun and which may well become part of the responsibility of the resident staff, is the theological training of those chosen as candidates for the non-stipendiary ministry.

Church Day Schools and the Education Board

The closing or transference of the day schools of the church is now almost complete. The Education Board has developed a series of other interests. The traditional attention to Sunday Schools and their teachers has continued. Educational work with children including residential courses and projects together with training courses for teachers are sponsored by the Board. Youth work, the support of the work of chaplains to students, adult religious education, and grants for ordinands are all part of the concern of the Board.

Overseas Missions

The traditional interest in the Diocese of St. John's in the Transkei, South Africa, continues. The Diocese of Nagpur is now part of the Church of North India. For many years grants have been made for the work in the Chanda Mission area in Nagpur diocese, and more recently such grants have gone to the diocese. It is expected that there will be a reduction in the support given in coming years. Other fields of missionary concern are also in the thoughts and the giving of churchpeople, and in particular New Guinea, Kuching, the work of the South American Missionary Society, and Mombasa. However, the list of such interest will continually change as the church seeks to respond to special needs. The list of priests and laypeople serving overseas in missionary situations includes workers in the diocese of St. John's, Cape Province, Malawi, Tanzania, Rhodesia, Zambia, Uganda, Burundi, Egypt, Israel, Mauritius, Malagasy, Nagpur, Calcutta, Delhi, Bihar, Nepal, Korea, New Guinea, Peru, Paraguay, Chile, and Guyana.

" Partners in Mission "

The Anglican Consultative Council issued the Report of its Second Meeting which was held in Dublin in 1973 under this title. It is an apt description of the role of the churches today and is relevant to the contemporary life of the Episcopal Church in Scotland in its relations with other churches. " The missionary task of the Church continues to be that of reconciling man to God, man to man, and man to his environment. There is but one mission in all the world, and this one mission is shared by the world-wide Christian community. The responsibility for mission in any place belongs to the church in that place."[1]

The decline in church membership and church attendance, the inflationary effects of the economic life of the community and their effect on the maintenance of church buildings, and the changing social conditions of the times have threatened the ability of many congregations to survive. At the same time a closer fellowship has been developing amongst Christians at parochial level. There is greater co-operation in some spheres of church life, and particularly in the field of social service. This is found in common action in Christian Aid activities. There is room for far more co-operation and a development of shared activities. Dialogue at official and unofficial levels with the Church of Scotland, the Roman Catholic Church in Scotland, and other Churches, has helped to break down some inherited prejudices.

Partnership in mission and service must open up many avenues of co-operation. The Social Service Board of the Church has always shown an awareness of the need for working with other

[1] Partners in Mission: Report of Anglican Consultative Council, Dublin.

churches and other agencies. The present range of its interests includes providing a professional casework service for unmarried mothers and others with personal and social problems. It runs an adoption society, and seeks to promote a sense of social responsibility among members of the church.

What does the future of the Episcopal Church in Scotland appear to be in the light of the present situation? It is perhaps easier to say than to define that its future can only be in terms of Mission, and that in partnership alongside other Christian communities in Scotland. If the role of the church is simply to provide the services of the Church of England for visitors from south of the border and thus to provide and maintain a number of " private chapels " for those who wish this, the closing of more and more churches and the virtual abandonment of any commitment to mission might be viewed with equanimity, or even seen as a desirable thing.

The Scottish Episcopal Church is often called " The English Church " by those who regard it thus simply as an alien church catering for visitors, and are happy to tolerate the existence of such a community. It must be acknowledged that the coming and going of clergy and people, Scottish, English, Irish, Welsh, and others, adds a great deal of richness to the traditions and the life of the church. There is a strong Scottish tradition. It is not desirable to attempt to assess the many strands of Scottish history and life which find expression as, for example in liturgcial tradition, in the forms of service and the practice of worshippers. The influences of the liturgical renewal inspired by the Oxford Movement are also clearly recognisable. The devotional life of many Scottish churchmen has been nourished by many traditions of spirituality. In many churches the Parish Communion is now the only well-attended Sunday Service.

Special features in church government include the election of Bishops by the Clerical and Lay Electors of the vacant diocese, the development of the Provincial Synod, and the growth and influence of the Representative Church Council. The history of these parts of the Scottish tradition link the church of today with its ancient roots in Scottish History.

Scottish churchmen of other churches are often surprised at the large element of lay participation in the councils of the Episcopal Church. A majority of lay as well as a majority of clerical electors is necessary for the election of a bishop. The Provincial Synod as now working has two houses, one of Bishops, and the other of clerical and lay members who are themselves elected as members by their Diocesan Councils or Synods. The Representative Church Council, and its Committees and Boards, consist of clerical and lay representatives. For one hundred years the Church Council has fulfilled an enabling service to the church, and has also on many occasions provided the forum for general discussion on matters which affect the well-being of the church and her work in the community.

If the Episcopal Church deserves to have any future it must be in terms of mission. An idea which is prevalent in these days is that, based on the principles of business management and accountancy, uneconomic units should be cut down and the number of clergy related to the " viable " remainder. This is not the way of mission and service. There can be no future in mission without sacrifice on the part of priest and people alike. Partnership in mission is an adventure into largely uncharted seas, an adventure which will be costly. The future of the church offers much that is exciting but there can be no easily defined " blue print ". Cardinal Suenens expressed it well in *The Future of the Christian Church:* " The Church is like a ship exposed to every wind and battling through a sort of Bay of Biscay. One reason for the situation has nothing to do with the ship, it is caused by the condition of the sea. The church exists in and for the world and as such lies open to the influence of the unprecedented changes which the world is experiencing. But there is also another reason, which belongs to the condition of the ship itself, not in some dry dock but out in the open sea."[1]

The Bishop of Moray wrote in the Annual Report of the Representative Church Council for 1973: " At present in our church there are groups of people who suggest that because we cannot get a nice neat and adequate dictionary definition of the meaning of mission in the 1970s we should all simply attend endless conferences and meetings to try to define it. In the meantime the church becomes more and more remote and introspective. We shall not discover what Home Mission means until we get out and start doing it. Our task is simply to make God ' real ' to his people. We do this by showing our loving zeal for God and the things of God and our no less loving care and concern for all his people—and that means those who acknowledge him and those who do not."

One course at least which it is not legitimate for the Episcopal Church to follow is that of failure to feel responsibility for the churchless thousands in the nation. There is a special part of this which must be felt and acknowledged, namely our duty to those who have lapsed from the church, but who still look to the Anglican Communion for spiritual guidance. There may be others who can be helped to a way of spirituality or an understanding of the faith through those experiences and insights which have come to us. It may be that partnership in mission requires from us an understanding of our task as a " tutor leading to Christ ". There is a continuing Home Mission work to bring into the living fellowship of the Church of Christ many who are outside its influence, and it may be that within this purpose there will also be discovered ways of ecumenical fellowship and sharing. It may be that priests will be appointed to work in ecumenical teams. It is likely that there will be need to build new churches in a number of centres, or it may be possible to share in the provision of community or shared churches.

[1] Ramsey and Suenens, *The Future of the Christian Church* (SCM 1971).

Admission to Holy Communion

The issue of admitting to Holy Communion those not confirmed who were members in good standing in other churches was fully discussed in the Provincial Synod and in Diocesan Synods, and also very widely throughout the church in 1968 and 1969. Problems of inter-communion were aired and considered. A Commission appointed by the Provincial Synod sent a questionnaire to clergy and laity and a summary of opinions was published. In its report to the Synod the Commission made a number of recommendations which were generally accepted by the Provincial Synod of 1969. These included the encouragement of Scottish Episcopalians to share in the worship (including the Eucharistic worship) of other Trinitarian Churches where they know that they are welcome to do so, recognising that some Episcopalians will then bear witness to their regard for truth and unity by abstaining from receiving Holy Communion, whilst other Episcopalians will then bear witness to their regard for truth and unity by accepting the invitation to receive Holy Communion. While general intercommunion was not considered acceptable, the Provincial Synod approved a recommendation " to refrain from passing judgment on those congregations and their clergy which, by virtue of their close association in mission with other Trinitarian Churches, participate according to conscience in each other's Eucharistic services from time to time when they know they are welcome to do so, effect always being given to the pastoral oversight of the Diocesan Bishop, acting in accordance with such directions as may be resolved upon by the College of Bishops." In reporting on the views of clergy and laity in his diocese, the Primus (Bishop Moncrieff) commented that in the ecumenical context there is a greater readiness to admit to Communion than there has been in the past. In suggesting a justification for this he said: " There is a greater sense of penitence about our divisions than a desire to persevere in them. Where there is a sincere intention to strive for unity the situation as between the Churches is altered. As a result of our common baptism into Christ we can regard each other as ' separated brethren ' in Him, and this makes admission to Communion more possible. Such admission should not be casual nor completely outside control or discipline.''

A new Canon, confirmed in 1965, on *Admitting to Holy Communion* affirmed the normal rule that those admitted to the Holy Communion be confirmed or ready and desirous to be confirmed. It also recognised that there are exceptions to the normal rule and remitted to the College of Bishops the framing of directions as to departures from it, provided that the causes are good and sufficient and not unacceptable to this Church generally.

Inter-church Relations
" A United Church of Scotland "

Reunion with the Church of Scotland in a reunited Church has been cherished by many Scottish Episcopalians for generations. Perhaps nothing has been so disappointing and frustrating in recent years as the search for such a relationship as would prepare the way for significant steps towards the reunion of these two churches. It was evident that the two churches were growing closer to one another in friendship and that differences of opinion and of theological judgment were on the whole not so much between the two churches as within each of them.

Discussions and conversations were so organised as to include the Church of England and the Presbyterian Church of England and thus the Church of Scotland and the Scottish Episcopal Church were brought into a larger area of consideration than that which concerned the situation in Scotland.

Conversations with the Church of Scotland

The first and second rounds of talks (1932–1934 and 1949–1951) were between the Church of Scotland and the Church of

England, at which representatives of the Scottish Episcopal Church and the Presbyterian Church of England were present. The third round of talks, from 1953, began with all four churches represented by full participants. A plan of union was proposed which included the mutual adaptation of the two Churches by introducing " bishops-in-presbytery " in the Church of Scotland and lay officers like elders in the Church of England. The Report was widely discussed in the press and by the Scottish public generally with very little sign of approval. The General Assembly of 1959 declared the proposals of the Report unacceptable. Professor Ian Henderson in *Power without Glory* wrote: " For two years the Bishops' Report controversy dragged on distracting the attention of the Church of Scotland from the vastly more important tasks of evangelising and adapting its approach to meet the situation created by the post-war industrial society. The proposals in the report introduced in Scottish ecclesiastical life an acrimony which had been absent from it for fifty years."[1]

The fourth round of talks was intended to be more restricted in that the General Assembly of 1959 laid down that before further progress could be made " certain issues require to be clarified and resolved . . . the chief among which concern (a) the meaning of unity as distinct from uniformity in Church Order (b) the meaning of ' validity ' as applied to ministerial orders (c) the doctrine of Holy Communion and (d) the meaning of the Apostolic Succession as related to all these matters." Representatives of the Church of England and the Scottish Episcopal Church asked that three additional questions be discussed namely, the Church as Royal Priesthood, the Place of the Laity in the Church, and the relations between Church, State and Community. It seemed that these talks were opening up a fruitful area of useful conversation which suggested ways of co operation and adaptation as would achieve a United Church of

[1] Ian Henderson, *Power without Glory*.

Scotland and a United Church of England. Alas, the hopes of many were disappointed and frustrated at the succession of failures and at the misrepresentations which abounded in the press and in public opinion.

The idea of covenanting together for unity seemed to some a way forward into a commitment which would draw the Churches more and more fully into partnership and in due course into unity. Clearly this was something to be discussed together with all its implications. It was a suggestion which some considered " useful ".

There was, however, strong opposition to the idea throughout the Church of Scotland where it was seen to be very dangerous. Professor Henderson discusses the suggestion from this point of view. He writes: " What it did was to take the Glasgow Regional Group's plan for episcopal ordination of all future Church of Scotland ministers and join this to the Nottingham Conference's idea of a binding covenant and a date for the one Church. The result was to put forward the concrete proposal that the Church of Scotland bind itself in a Covenant to unite with the Scottish Episcopal Church under bishops in fifteen years' time."

The argument dragged on. There is no purpose in attempting to go beyond observing that what seemed a helpful suggestion quickly grew into an imaginary plot to " take over " the Church of Scotland.

Since then conversations have continued without reaching any hopeful stage though at local level many in both churches are seeking to understand one another and to discover ways of working and worshipping together.

The prospects of a United Church of Scotland are not bright. In 1971, following conversations between representatives of the Church of Scotland and the Episcopal Church in Scotland there came a suggestion that the Episcopal Church should become a non-territorial synod of the Church of Scotland. The Provincial

Synod discussed the idea sympathetically but rejected it. The General Assembly in May 1974 declared its opposition to a proposal to have superintendents in a united church of the future. In presenting the report on the current Multilateral Conversations the Convener of the Committee added that his committee believed there was no possibility of the system of government associated with superintendents being accepted by the Church of Scotland. The Revd. Andrew Herron, a former Moderator of the General Assembly, added to the discussion: "This brings us close to the real issue that divides us all the way through, the question of apostolic succession and bishops." In his book, *Record Apart*, Mr Herron writes: "Either you believe that authority within the Church vests in individuals set apart and ordained within the Apostolic succession for the sole purpose, within God's inscrutable design, of bearing that rule, or else you believe in a conciliar form of Church government and see the minister, answering to his presbytery, as carrying the highest powers within the Church. You can say, as Anglicans seem to say, that without bishops of that sort there can be no church and in so saying find you have un-churched those with whom you are conversing: or you can say, as we do, that your system is ' conformable to the Word of God ' and so pass judgment upon none. What you cannot do is simultaneously to say both."[1]

Joint Study with Representatives of the Roman Catholic Church

The discussions which have taken place between representatives of the Scottish Episcopal Church and representatives of the Roman Catholic Church in Scotland have issued in common statements on " The Nature of Baptism and its place in the Life of the Church " and " The Ecclesial Nature of the Eucharist ". Both statements indicate a large measure of agreement. The relations of friendship already established have helped to remind Episcopalians of the many changes which have taken place within the Roman

[1] Andrew Herron, *Record Apart.*

Catholic Church of recent years. Rome has adopted many of the insights of the Reformation: services in the vernacular, the primacy of the individual conscience, the open Bible, the participation of laity in the divine service, and to some extent, communion in both kinds. Further study on " The Ministry " and " Intercommunion " is proposed. " We know very well that the nearer we move to the practical implications of our agreement on the centrality of our faith, the closer we come to the problems of entrenched positions and attitudes of mind rooted in history rather than reason."[1]

Multilateral Conversations

The interim Report of Multilateral Church Conversations in Scotland (1972) offers a wide-ranging field of discussion on controlling principles for a basis of union among Scottish Churches. The churches represented include Churches of Christ, the Church of Scotland, the Congregational Union, the Methodist Synod, the United Free Church and the Scottish Episcopal Church. It was considered that in seeking unity it was necessary to seek a common mind on the Mission of the Church, the changes which seemed to be necessary in the structure and methods of the Scottish Churches for the better understanding of their mission in Scotland, and the various kinds of Ministry best suited to the fulfilment of this mission.[1]

The report is being discussed and it is therefore too soon to estimate its significance for the future.

" Partners in Mission " in the context of the discussion in church relations in Scotland leads the writer to think about the task and the problem along lines very familiar to Scottish Episcopalian Churchmen for generations. One may have sympathy with the Roman Catholic Bishop who advocates a keen interest in ecumenism with the stricture " that no Catholic has any

[1] *Ecclesial Nature of the Eucharist: Report of Joint Study Group.*
[2] *Multilateral Church Conversation: Interim Report.*

right to be interested in ecumenism who is not deeply committed to his own church in faith and practice ". As of the
Anglican Communion, so of the Scottish Episcopal Church, a
significant part of her contribution to a United Church involves
faithfulness to the traditions of evangelical truth and apostolic
order. The Anglican " Via Media " in theology and practice
may be as necessary to the progress of any movement towards
Christian Unity as in the days of Richard Hooker or Bishop
Andrewes. The Scottish Episcopal Church has need to re
consider her mission, while still seeking to find and use every
opportunity of partnership. Perhaps in her search she will find
a new and worthy role.

The Provincial Synod

The Provincial Synod of 1960 made a major change in the role
and membership of the Synod when it brought to an end the
Consultative Council on Church Legislation and provided for an
enlarged Provincial Synod which, in addition to the Bishops,
Deans and certain others, provided for the election of clerical
and lay members. The calling of the Synod is now a regular
matter and not simply an occasional one when canonical changes
are discussed or proposed. The Bishops may consult with the
Synod at any time on any matter on which they wish their
counsel. Inter-church relations have been much to the fore and
many of the changes made in the Canons themselves bear witness
to a desire to assist the church in adapting to a changed ecumenical climate, and especially in showing itself more hospitable
to those outside its membership. Thus ministers of other
churches may be permitted to assist at certain services, and to
preach.

A number of changes and additions were approved to the
services of the Scottish Prayer Book, and the Scottish Liturgy in
re-arranged form, incorporating some of the permitted changes
and, thus authorised by the College of Bishops, under a power of

dispensation granted to it by the Provincial Synod, has been in general use since 1970. This fairly conservative revision is commonly known as " The Grey Book ".

The Canon " Of the Election of Bishops " has been revised so as to incorporate certain changes in procedure, but no change in any point of principle. The election is still made by the Clerical and Lay Electors of the vacant diocese. A list of names is compiled on the suggestion of the electors. The College of Bishops is now also permitted to submit to the dean not more than three possible names. All these names, with factual particulars about each of them, are then circulated to all electors before the electoral meeting. If any new name is then suggested and a fifth of the electors are willing to allow the name to be considered, there is to be an adjournment to give time for careful consideration. The former procedure is maintained at the election, proposing, seconding and voting.

A considerable amount of tidying up of the Code of Canons was done in a general revision, and this revised Code, incorporating amendments made since 1929, was published in 1973.[1]

Varieties of Ministry

A report of a commission to the Provincial Synod under this title discussed the varieties of ministry in the church, and suggested that there is an important and probably increasing role to be found within the ordained ministry for deacons and priests whose income is derived from secular employment. The view was expressed that any scheme for the use as well as for the training of such a ministry must be of great flexibility " and yet worked out in sufficient detail to enable the Church at large to understand what is proposed and have confidence in it ".[2] Some regard the development of the non-stipendiary ministry as an important ingredient in a new strategy of mission.

[1] *Code of Canons of the Episcopal Church*, in Scotland.
[2] *Varieties of Ministry : A Report.*

The increasing cost of maintaining and caring for church buildings, and the doubts as to the ability of the church to support as many full-time clergy as in former years tends too often to suggest closing churches, or simply arranging a convenient " linking " arrangement, or a " grouping " of congregations. Adjustments and amalgamations may often seem the necessary answer to the problem of costs. It is not likely in itself to make the church more missionary. Yet within " groups " of churches there may well be scope for teams of clergy including full-time and non-stipendiary deacons or priests. Is this the shape of the ministry in the years to come?

The Episcopal Church has known for many years the value of the Lay Reader who holds a licence from the Bishop to preach, conduct services (other than those of a sacramental nature) and to visit the sick and others.

A number of priests who have served in the full-time ministry for some years, later take up secular employment (often teaching posts) and continue to give some assistance to the church either as honorary curates taking charge of congregations, or by providing occasional duty when called upon.

Several men have been ordained, and others are likely to be ordained, while continuing their secular work.

The church needs full-time priests who are equipped for the role they will be required to undertake in the coming years. Theirs will be a positive contribution to the formation and training of groups and they will require gifts of leadership. The training and the equipment of both the full-time clergy and non-stipendiary clergy of the future will have an important bearing on the development of the church in her mission in the coming decades.

In the changes of recent decades there seem to be trends which give promise of help to the Church in its work, and yet may contain in themselves hidden dangers.

The mood of the Church at present seems increasingly

favour of centralisation. One strong centre, it is held, can cope better with the machinery of administration than a number of smaller, less well-equipped centres. It would be a pity, however, if such a tendency should take away or undermine that strong congregational independence, which in the past developed in each local church a sturdy desire to be, as far as possible, self-supporting. Congregational histories bear witness to the strenuous efforts made by congregations to meet their own building costs, to support their own incumbent, and yet to make their contributions to the general work of the Church, at home and overseas. How much of this generous spirit of local loyalty would be taken away if the diocese, for example, had complete administrative control over the charges, and a decisive voice on what the local church is to contribute financially, and how it is to be spent? A central committee, or a diocesan one, however expert, may be remote from the situation which it is seeking to assess.

It is important not to under-value the witness of the individual congregation, its independence and its friendly relation with other nearby churches. In considering the task of the church in the world, the Bishops at the Lambeth Conference in 1948 declared, " The Church in the diocese and parish is the key to the whole situation. The local congregation is the place where men must find the life of the great Church, which is God's instrument for the world's salvation. See to it, then, that your congregation is a true community in Christ, that it may influence the common life of its whole neighbourhood."[1]

Looking Forward

In an age of lawlessness and permissiveness, and in a time when the economic climate seems to deal harsh blows on the church's administrative work and the maintenance of her buildings it is far from easy to see clearly through " the encircling gloom ".

[1] *Report of Lambeth Conference*, 1948.

Yet the eye of faith does see and in its sight lies the call to be faithful and to bear witness to the things that are not merely temporal. The Church is in great need of such a grasp of her mission that she will be ready and alert to find ways and means of proclaiming her message and living her life. Her missionary outreach will assuredly be in partnership with other Christian communities. There is a special role of teaching and sharing to be carried forward. Within this an important element is that of a spirituality which can draw from the treasures of the past and still be relevant to the needs of the present age. A part of partnership in mission is in the life of prayer and worship.

Arguments, conflicts, and disagreements seem to have marked the relations of churches in Scotland in the past. Is there a way of discovering, in prayer and worship and in working together, that we need each other if we are to reach that truth which is more than any of our churches has fully grasped or can understand in isolation?

It was observed of a church building of architectural merit in Glasgow: " During the time various interests fought over its future, vandals fought over its present, and so it has no future." There is a spirit of vandalism at large in contemporary society. There is all the more need for the church to be fully engaged in its work for the redemption of society, for this is her mission and her duty. The Scottish Episcopal Church and its future must be seen in relation to the whole Catholic Church set in the world, and under the judgment of the Gospel. Within this she has an important part as the representative of the family of Anglican Churches in full communion with each other.

APPENDIX A: EXTRACT FROM A LETTER FROM BISHOP ROSE TO BISHOP CAMPBELL (22 OCTOBER 1713)

SEVERAL references are made in Chapter Three to the letter written by Bishop Rose of Edinburgh to Bishop Campbell, one of the College Bishops, in 1713. This letter has been preserved at the Theological College, Edinburgh.[1] The following extract describes the visit of Bishop Rose to London at the Revolution in 1688:

" When in October 1688, the Scots Bishops came to know of the intended invasion by the Prince of Orange, a good many of them being then at Edinburgh, meeting together, concerted and sent up a loyal address to the king. Afterwards, in November, finding that the prince was landed, and foreseeing the dreadful convulsions that were like to ensue, and not knowing what damages might arise from thence, both to the church and state, resolved to send up two of their number to the king, with a renewed tender of their duty; instructing them also to wait on the bishops of England, for advice and assistance, in case that any unlucky thing might possibly happen to occur with respect to the church. This resolution being taken, it was represented by the two archbishops to his majesty's privy council and was agreed to and approven by them; whereupon, at the next meeting of the bishops, it was not thought fit, even by the archbishops themselves, that any of them (though they were the men of the greatest ability and experience) should go up, as being less acceptable to the English bishops from their having consented to the taking off the sanguinary laws against Papists, and so that undertaking was devolved over upon Dr. Bruce, bishop of Orkney, and me, he having suffered for not agreeing to that

[1] P.E.C.S., No. 1833. In the extract below I have modernized the spelling of some words.

project, and I not concerned as not being a bishop at that time
And, accordingly, a commission was drawn and signed for us two
the 3d of December 1688. The bishop of Orkney promisin
to come back from the country in eight or ten days time, that w
might journey together, occasioned my stay: But when that tim
was elapsed, I had a letter from him, signifying that he had falle
very ill, and desiring me to go up post so soon as I could, promisin
to follow as soon as his health could serve. Whereupon I too
post; and in a few days coming to Northallerton, where, hearin
of the king's having left Rochester, I stood doubtful with mysel
whether to go forward or return: But considering the variou
and contradictory accounts I had got all along upon the road, an
that, in case of the king's retirement, matters would be so muc
more dark and perplexed, I resolved to go on, that I might be abl
to give just accounts of things to my brethren here from time t
time, and have the advice of the English bishops, whom I neve
doubted to find unalterably firm to their master's interest
And so this was the occasion of my coming to London, so, b
reason of the bishop of Orkney's illness, that difficult task fell t
my share alone.

"The very next day after my arrival at London, I waited o
the archbishop of Canterbury, and after my presenting, and h
Grace's reading of my commission, his Grace said, that matte
were very dark, and the cloud so thick or gross that they coul
not see through it: They know not well what to do for them
selves, and far less what advice to give to me; but there was t
be a meeting of the bishops with him that very day, and desired m
to see him the week thereafter. I then waited on the the
bishop of St. Asaph's, who treated me in such a manner that
could not but see through his inclinations; wherefore I resolve
to visit him no more, nor to address myself to any others of th
order, till I should have occasion to learn something further abo
them: Wherefore the week thereafter I repaired to Lambeth
and told his Grace all that had past betwixt St. Asaph and m

who, smiling, replied that St. Asaph was a good man, but an angry man; and withal told me, that matters still continued dark, and that it behoved me to wait the issue of their convention, which he suspected was only that which would give light, and open the scene; and withal desired me to come to him from time to time, and if anything occurred he would signify it unto me.

"In that wearisome season, I waited on the bishop of London and entreated him to speak to the prince to put a stop to the persecutions of our clergy; but to no purpose. I was also with the then Dr. Burnet upon the same design, but with the same success, who told me, that he did not meddle in Scots affairs. I was also earnestly desired by the bishop of London, and the then viscount of Tarbet, and some other Scots peers, to wait upon the prince, and present him with an address upon that head. I asked, whether I or my address would readily meet with acceptance or success, if it did not compliment the prince upon his descent to deliver us from Papacy and slavery? They said, that that was absolutely necessary. I told, that I neither was instructed by my constituents to do so, neither had I myself clearness to do it; and that in these terms I neither could nor would either visit or address his Highness. In that season, also, I had the honour to be acquainted and to be several times with the worthy Dr. Turner, the then bishop of Ely, whose conversation was very useful to me, and every way agreeable; and besides these bishops already mentioned, I had not the honour to be acquainted with any other. And thus the whole time of the convention passed off, excepting what was spent in necessary duties and visiting our countrymen, even until the day that the dark scene opened, by the surprising vote of abdication, on which very day I went over to Lambeth; and what passed there betwixt his Grace and me (being all in private) it is both needless, would be very tedious, and perchance not so very proper to write it. In the close, I told his Grace, that I would make ready to go home, and only wait upon his Grace once more before I took my journey.

" While I was making my visits of leave to my countrymen, I was surprisingly told that some two or three of them, attempting to go home without passes, were the first stage stopped on the road, and that none were to expect passes without waiting upon the prince: Whereupon I repaired again to Lambeth to have his Grace's advice, who, considering the necessity of that compliment, agreed to my making of it. Upon my applying to the bishop of London (Compton) to introduce me, his Lordship asked me, whether I had anything to say to the king? (so was the style in England then.) I replied, that I had nothing to say, save that I was going for Scotland, being a member of the Convention, for I understood that without waiting on the prince, (that being the most common Scots style,) I could not have a pass, and that without that I must needs be stopped upon the road, as severals of my countrymen had been. His Lordship asked me again, saying, seeing your clergy have been, and are so barbarously treated by the Presbyterians, will you not speak to the king to put a stop to that, and in favours of your own clergy? My reply was, that the prince had been often applied to in that matter by severals of our nobility, and addressed also by the sufferers themselves, and yet to no purpose: wherefore I could have no hopes that my intercessions would be of any avail; but that if his Lordship thought otherways, I would not decline to make them. His Lordship asked me further, whether any of our countrymen would go along with me, and he spoke particularly of Sir George Mackenzie. I replied, that I doubted nothing of that: Whereupon his Lordship bid me find him out, and that both he and I should be at court that day against three in the afternoon, and he should surely be there to introduce us. All which I (having found Sir George,) imparted to him, who liked it well, and said it was a good occasion; but wished that severals of our nobility might be advertised by us to be there also. To which I replied, that I doubted much whether coming in a body to the prince he would give us access, and that our nobility would be much offended at us, if coming to court upon our invitation, access should be denied them; and therefore I thought it best that we alone should meet the bishop at the time appointed, and advise with him what was fit to be done, which was agreed to; and upon our meeting with the bishop, Sir George made that overture to his Lordship, which he closing with very warmly, said, he would go in to the king, and see if he would appoint a time for the Scots Episcopal nobility and gentry to wait upon him in favours of the clergy of Scotland so sadly persecuted. Whereupon the bishop leaving us in a room of Whitehall, near adjoining to the place where the prince was, stayed about a half-hour from us; and upon his return told us, that the king's answer was, that he would not allow us to come to him in a body, lest that might give jealousy and umbrage to the Presbyterians; neither would he permit them (for the same reason) to come to him in numbers; and that he would not allow above two of either party at a time to speak to him in church matters.

" Then the bishop, directing his discourse to me, said, My Lord, you see that the king, having thrown himself upon the water, must keep himself a-swimming with one hand; the Presbyterians having joined him closely, and offer to support him; and therefore he cannot cast them off, unless he could see how otherways he can be served. And the king bids me tell you, that he now knows the state of Scotland much better than he did when he was in Holland; for, while there, he was made believe that Scotland generally all over was Presbyterian, but now he sees that the great body of the nobility and gentry are for Episcopacy, and 'tis the trading and inferior sort that are for Presbytery: wherefore he bids me tell you, that if you will undertake to serve him to the purpose that he is served here in England, he will take you by the hand, support the Church and Order, and throw off the Presbyterians. My answer to this was, My Lord, I cannot but humbly thank the prince for this frankness and offer; but withal I must tell your Lordship, that, when I came from Scotland, neither my brethren nor I apprehended any such revolution as I have now seen in England; and therefore I never was, nor could be, instructed by them what answer to make to the prince's offer: And therefore what I say is not in their name, but only my private opinion, which is, that I truly think they will not serve the prince so as he is served in England, that is, (as I take it) to make him their king, or give their suffrage for his being king. And though as to this matter I can say nothing in their name, and as from them, yet for myself I must say, that, rather than do so, I will abandon all the interest that either I have or may expect to have in Britain. Upon that the bishop commended my openness and ingenuity, and said he believed it was so; for, says he, all this time you have been here, neither have you waited on the king, nor have any of your brethren the Scots bishops made any address to him. So the king must be excused for standing by the Presbyterians.

" Immediately upon this the prince, going somewhere abroad, came through our room; and Sir George Mackenzie takes leave of him in very few words. I applied to the bishop, and said, My Lord, there is now no farther place for application in our church matters, and this opportunity of taking leave of the prince is lost; wherefore I beg that your Lordship would introduce me for that effect, if you can, next day about ten or eleven in the forenoon; which his Lordship both promised and performed. And upon my being admitted to the prince's presence, he came three or four steps forward from his company, and prevented me, by saying, My Lord, are you going for Scotland? My reply was, Yes, Sir, if you have any commands for me. Then he said, I hope you will be kind to me, and follow the example of England. Wherefore being somewhat difficulted how to make a mannerly and discreet answer without entangling myself, I readily replied, Sir, I will serve you so far as law, reason, or conscience shall allow me. How this answer pleased I cannot well tell, but it seems the limitations and conditions of it were not acceptable, for instantly the prince, without saying anything more, turned away from me and went back to his company. Considering what had passed the day before, I was much surprised to find the prince accost me in those terms; but I presume, that either the bishop (not having time) had not acquainted him with what had passed, or that the prince purposed to try what might be made of me by the honour he did me of that immediate demand. And as that was the first, so it was the last time I had the honour to speak with his Highness, when the things I now write were not only upon the matter, but in the self-same individual words that I have set them down.

" Whether what the bishop of London delivered as from the prince was so or not, I cannot certainly say, but I think his Lordship's word was good enough for that; or whether the prince would have stood by his promise of casting off the Presbyterians and protecting us, in case we had come into his interest, I will not determine, though this seems the most probable unto me: and that for these reasons, he had the Presbyterians sure on his side, both from inclination and interest, many of them having come over with him, and the rest of them having appeared so warmly, that with no good grace imaginable could they return to King James's interest: Next, by gaining, as he might presume to gain, the Episcopal nobility and gentry, which he saw was a great party, and consequently that King James would be deprived of his principal support: Then he saw what a hardship it would be upon the Church of England, and of what bad consequence to see Episcopacy ruined in Scotland, who, no doubt, would have vigorously interposed for us, if we, by our carriage, could have been brought to justify their measures. And I am the more confirmed in this, that, after my downcoming here, my Lord St. Andrews and I taking occasion to wait upon the Duke Hamilton, his Grace told us a day or two before the sitting down of the convention, that he had it in special charge from King William, that nothing should be done to the prejudice of Episcopacy in Scotland, in case the bishops could by any means be brought to befriend his interest, and prayed us most pathetically, for our own sake, to follow the example of the Church of England. To which my Lord St. Andrews replied, That both by natural allegiance, the laws, and the most solemn oaths, we were engaged in the king's interest, and that we were by God's grace to stand by it in the face of all dangers, and to the greatest losses: subjoining, that his Grace's quality and influence did put it in his hands to do his master the greatest service, and himself the surest honour; and if he acted otherways, it might readily lie as a heavy task and curse both upon himself and his family.''

APPENDIX B: BISHOPS OF THE TWENTIETH CENTURY

ABERDEEN AND ORKNEY

Rowland Ellis (1906–1911): After service in his native Wales he was appointed Rector of St. Paul's Edinburgh, and was Synod Clerk of the Diocese of Edinburgh when elected to Aberdeen.

Anthony Mitchell (1912–1917): Rector of St. Andrew's, Glasgow, and Principal of the Church's Theological College, Edinburgh. Anthony Mitchell was a distinguished churchman and historian. He wrote a history of the Episcopal Church in Scotland. His *Biographical Studies in Scottish Church History* deserves to be more widely known.

Frederic Llewellyn Deane (1917–1943): Formerly Vicar in Leicester, and Provost of St. Mary's Cathedral, Glasgow.

Herbert William Hall (1943–1955): Formerly Rector of Port Glasgow, Galashiels and Portobello, and organiser for Scotland of the Home Mission Appeal launched in 1934.

Edward Frederick Easson (1956–1972): Formerly mission priest in Edinburgh, rector of Peterhead and Bieldside. He was Dean of Aberdeen when elected Bishop.

Iain Forbes Begg (1973–   ): Formerly mission priest at Seaton, Aberdeen, and Dean of the Diocese.

ARGYLL AND THE ISLES

Kenneth Mackenzie (1907–1942): Formerly Rector and Provost of St. Paul's Cathedral, Dundee.

Thomas Hannay (1942–1962, and Primus from 1952): Formerly a mission priest with U.M.C.A. and Principal of the Theological College, Mirfield.

Richard Knyvet Wimbush (1963–   , and Primus from 1974): Formerly Chaplain of Cuddesdon Theological College, Rector of

Melsonby, Yorks., and Principal of Edinburgh Theological College.

BRECHIN

Walter John Robberds (1904–1935, and Primus from 1908): Formerly Chaplain of Cuddesdon Theological College, Rector of Arbroath, and Vicar of St. Mary Redcliffe, Bristol.

Kenneth Donald Mackenzie (1935–1943): Formerly Dean and Chaplain of Pembroke College, Oxford, and Vicar of Selly Oak, and Richmond.

Eric Graham (1944–1959): Formerly Vice-Principal at Sarum Theological College, and Principal of Cuddesdon Theological College.

John Chappell Sprott (1959–1975): After serving as a priest in Glasgow and London, he became Provost of St. Paul's Cathedral, Dundee.

Lawrence Edward Luscombe (1975–   ): After serving as a priest in Glasgow, he became Provost of St. Paul's Cathedral, Dundee.

EDINBURGH

George Henry Somerset Walpole (1910–1929): Formerly succentor at Truro Cathedral and tutor at the Theological College, incumbent of Auckland Cathedral, New Zealand, and head of the Theological College, Professor of Systematic Theology in the General Theological Seminary, New York, Principal of Bede College, Durham, and Vicar of Lambeth Parish Church.

Harry Seymour Reid (1929–1939): He served his whole ministry in Edinburgh, and was successively Rector of St. Mark's, St. Paul's, and St. Cuthbert's. He was Dean of the Diocese for ten years before his election to the Bishopric.

Ernest Denny Logie Danson (1939–1947, and Primus from 1943): Formerly Chaplain at Singapore, Java, and Negri Sembilan,

Bishop of Labuan and Sarawak, Assistant Bishop of Carlisle and Provost of St. Mary's Cathedral, Edinburgh.

Kenneth Charles Harman Warner (1947–1961): Formerly an R.A.F. Chaplain, Provost of St. Mary's Cathedral, Glasgow, and Archdeacon of Lincoln.

Kenneth Moir Carey (1961–1975): Formerly Vicar of Spennymoor, and Principal of Westcott House, Cambridge.

GLASGOW AND GALLOWAY

Archibald Ean Campbell (1904–1921): Formerly Vicar of Castle Rising, Norfolk, All Souls, Leeds, and Provost of St. Ninian's Cathedral, Perth.

Edward Thomas Scott Reid (1921–1931): Formerly Rector of Hawick, and St. Bride's, Glasgow. Translated to St. Andrews.

John Russell Darbyshire (1931–1938): Formerly Chaplain and Vice-Principal of Ridley Hall, Cambridge, Vicar of St. Luke's, Liverpool, and Archdeacon of Sheffield. After seven years in Glasgow he became Archbishop of Capetown.

John Charles Halland How (1938–1952, and Primus from 1946): Formerly Lecturer on Hebrew at St. John's and Trinity Colleges, Cambridge, Diocesan Missioner in Manchester, Rector of Liverpool and Vicar of Brighton.

Francis Hamilton Moncrieff (1952–1974, and Primus from 1962): Formerly Rector of St. Salvador's, Edinburgh, and Diocesan Missioner, Edinburgh.

Frederick Goldie (1974–   ): Formerly Rector at Hillington, Dumbarton, and St. Margaret's, Glasgow. Lecturer at Edinburgh Theological College, Dean of Glasgow and Galloway.

MORAY, ROSS AND CAITHNESS

Arthur John Maclean (1904–1943, and Primus from 1935): Formerly Chaplain at Cumbrae, Rector at Selkirk, Principal of Edinburgh Theological College.

Piers Holt Wilson (1943–1952): Formerly Rector of All Saints, St. Andrews.

Duncan Macinnes (1953–1970): Formerly Curate in charge of Knightswood, and Rector of Glencoe.

George Minshull Sessford (1970–   ): Formerly Curate in charge of Cumbernauld, and Rector of Forres.

ST. ANDREWS, DUNKELD AND DUNBLANE

Charles Edward Plumb (1908–1930): Formerly tutor at St. Aidan's College, Birkenhead, Principal of St. Stephen's House, Oxford, Rector of Braemar, and Provost of St. Ninian's Cathedral, Perth.

Edward Thomas Scott Reid (1931–1939): Formerly Bishop of Glasgow and Galloway (see previous entry).

James Lumsden Barkway (1939–1949): Formerly Vicar of Christ Church, Luton, Rector of Gaddesden, and Bishop Suffragan of Bedford.

Arnold Brian Burrowes (1950–1955): Formerly Fellow, Lecturer, Dean and Chaplain of Pembroke College, Oxford, and Principal of Sarum Theological College.

John William Alexander Howe (1955–1969): Formerly Chaplain Adisadel College, Ghana, and Vice-Principal of Edinburgh Theological College. Later Secretary General of the Anglican Consultative Council.

Michael Geoffrey Hare-Duke (1969–   ): Formerly Vicar of St. Mark's, Bury, and Vicar of St. Paul's, Daybrook, Nottingham.

BIBLIOGRAPHY

Chiefly authorities to which reference is made in the text and notes.

Acts of General Assemblies (abbr. *Acts G.A.*). 1560–1618; 1638–1842.
Acts of Parliament, Scotland (abbr. *Acts P.S.*).
Acts of Parliament of William III.
Arnot, Hugo, *Criminal Trials.* 1785.

Baillie, Robert, *Letters and Journals*, 3 vols. 1842.
Balcanqual, Dean, *Large Declaration.* 1639.
Ball, T. I., *A. Chinnery-Haldane, A Pastoral Bishop.* 1907.
Blatch, W., *Life of Bishop Low.* 1855.
Boswell, James, *Tour to the Hebrides.* 1786.
Buchan, John, *Montrose.* 1928.
Burnet, G., *History of His Own Time*, 4 vols. 1815.
  Vindication of Church and State in Scotland. 1673.
Butler, D., *Life and Letters of Robert Leighton.* 1903.

Calderwood, D., *History of the Kirk of Scotland*, 7 vols. 1842.
Campbell, Bishop Archibald Ean: A Memoir, edited by G. T. S. Farquhar. 1921.
Canons of the Episcopal Church in Scotland, in particular 1811, 1828, 1838,
  1863, 1876, 1890, 1911, 1929, and 1973.
Carlyle, Alex, of Inveresk, *Autobiography.* 1860.
Carslaw, W. H., *Life of James Renwick.* 1893.
Chambers, R., *Domestic Annals of Scotland*, 3 vols. 1858–61.
Church Society Annual Reports, 1838–1875.
Cleland, Jas., *Annals of Glasgow, being an account of the rise and progress of Glasgow.*
  1816.
Cook, George, *History of the Church of Scotland.* 1815.
Craven, J. B., *History of the Episcopal Church in Moray.* 1889.
  Records of the Dioceses of Argyll and the Isles. 1907.
  History of the Church in Orkney. 1883.
Cunningham, John, *History of the Church of Scotland*, 2 vols. 1859.

Don, Alan C., *The Scottish Book of Common Prayer, 1929.* 1949.
Donaldson, M. E. M., *Scotland's Suppressed History.* 1935.
  Till Scotland Melts in Flame. 1949.
Dowden, John, *The Annotated Scottish Communion Office.* 1884.

Evelyn, John, *Diary* (1620–1706), edited by A. Dobson. 1906.

Farquhar, G. T. S., *Three Bishops of Dunkeld.* 1915.
  Episcopal History of Perth. 1894.

Garden, George, "Life of Dr. John Forbes", prefixed *Opera Omnia*, the Works
  of Dr. Forbes. 1702.
Gordon, Jas. (of Rothiemay), *Scots Affairs*, 3 vols., pub. by the Spalding Club.
  1841.
Gordon, Jas., *The Reformed Bishop.* 1679.
Grub, George, *Ecclesiastical History of Scotland.* 1861.

Henderson, G. D., *Religious Life in Seventeenth Century Scotland*. 1937.
Historical Relation of the General Assembly of 1690. 1691.
Holland, H. Scott, *George Howard Wilkinson, Bishop*.

James the Sixth, *Basilikon Doron*. 1599.

Keith, R., *History of the Affairs of Church and State*. 1734.
    Historical Catalogue of the Scottish Bishops, edited by M. Russell. 1824.
Kerr, Jas., *The Covenants and the Covenanters*. 1895.
Kirkton, J., *Secret History of the Church of Scotland*, edited by C. K. Sharpe. 1817.
Knox, Bp. E., *Robert Leighton, a study of his life, times and writings*. 1930.
Knox, John, *History of the Reformation of the Church in Scotland*, edited by Laing. 1846.

Lang, Andrew, *History of Scotland*, 4 vols. 1907.
Lathbury, T., *History of the Non-Jurors*. 1843.
Lawson, J. P., *History of the Scottish Episcopal Church*. 1843.
Lecky, W. E. H., *History of England during the 18th Century*, 2 vols. 1878.
Lee, Robert, *Reform of the Church of Scotland*. 1864.
Lindsay, R., *True Narrative of the Proceedings in the Perth Assembly*, 4 vols. 1621.
Lockhart of Carnwath, *Papers*, 2 vols. 1817.
Luckock, H. M., *The Church in Scotland*. 1893.
Lyon, C. J., *History of St. Andrews*. 1843.

Mackenzie, Agnes M., *The Scotland of Queen Mary and the Religious Wars (1513–1638)*. 1936.
    The Kingdom of Scotland. 1940.
Macmillan, D., *The Aberdeen Doctors, Scottish Theologians, 1610–1638*. 1909.
MS. Memoirs of the Episcopal Church in Scotland (P.E.C.S.). 1738.
MS. Register of the College of Bishops (P.E.C.S.).
Mason, A. J., *George Howard Wilkinson*, 2 vols. 1909.
Melville, James, *Diary*, published 1829.
Mitchell, A., *Scotland's Church* (rev.). 1933.
    Biographical Studies in Scottish Church History. 1914.
Morer, T., *Short Account of Scotland*. 1702.
Mowat, J. D., *Scottish Church History*. 1939.

Neale, J. M., *Life of Bishop Torry*. 1856.

Papers of the Episcopal Church in Scotland (abbr. P.E.C.S.).
Parliamentary History of England, 36 vols. Hansard, 1806–20.
Pearson, J. N., *Life of Archbishop Leighton*. 1835.
Pepys, S., *Diary*, ed. by Lord Braybrooke. 1875.
Perry, W., *The Oxford Movement in Scotland*. 1932.
    George Hay Forbes. 1927.
    Alexander Penrose Forbes, the Scottish Pusey. 1939.
    Anthony Mitchell, Bishop. 1920.
    The Scottish Liturgy, its value and history. 1922.
    The Scottish Prayer Book. 1941.
Perry, W. S., *History of the American Episcopal Church*. 1885.
Peterkin, Alex, *Booke of the Universal Kirk of Scotland*. 1838.

Remains of Bishop Sandford, with Memoir by John Sandford. 1830.
Representation of the State of the Church in North Britain (MS. amongst P.E.C.S.). 1718.

BIBLIOGRAPHY

Representative Church Council Annual Reports, 1876–1974.
Ross, A. J., *Memoir of Bishop Ewing.* 1877.
Rothes, Lord, *Relation of Proceedings.* 1830.
Russell, M., " Life of Spottiswood ", prefixed to the 1850 ed. of Spottiswood's *History.*

Scots Magazine, passim.
Scott, H., *Fasti Ecclesiae Scoticanae.* 1866.
Scottish Chronicle, passim.
Scottish Churchman, passim.
Scottish Ecclesiastical Journal, passim.
Scottish Guardian, passim.
Sinclair, Sir John, *Statistical Account of Scotland.* 1826.
Skinner, John, *Ecclesiastical History of Scotland.* 1788.
Skinner, Dean John, *The Annals of the Episcopal Church in Scotland.* 1818.
Snow, W. G. S., *Bishop Harrison.* 1949.
 Arthur John Maclean, Bishop and Primus. 1950.
Somerville, T., *History of the Reign of Queen Anne.* 1798.
Spalding Club, *Miscellany*, 34 vols. 1841–1871.
 Historical Papers relating to the Jacobite Period.
Spottiswood, John, *History of the Church of Scotland.* 1668.
Stanhope, Lord, *Life of Pitt.* 1861.
Stephen, T., *History of the Church of Scotland.* 1845.
Stephen, W., *History of the Scottish Church.* 1896.
Stewart, D., *Sketches of the Highlands.* 1822.
Symson, P., *Present State of Scotland.* 1634.

Walker, W., *Bishop George Gleig.* 1878.
 John Skinner, of Linshart. 1883.
 Bishop Alexander Jolly. 1878.
 Bishop John Skinner. 1887.
 Three Churchmen, Bishops Russell and Terrot and Professor Grub. 1893.
Wilberforce, Bp., *History of the American Church.* 1846.
Wodrow, R., *History of the Sufferings of the Church of Scotland.* 1721.
 Correspondence. 1842.
Wordsworth, Charles, *Annals of my Life.* 1893.
 Scottish Church History from the Reformation. 1881.

* The Papers of the Episcopal Church in Scotland are kept in the Theological College of the Province, in Edinburgh. Besides the MSS. noted in the Bibliography, the Papers include letters written by the Bishops of the Church during the 17th and 18th centuries, dealing with such questions as the Usages, the Non-Jurors in England, the state of the disestablished Church, the consecration of Bishops to maintain the succession, and the office of Primus. The Papers also include the following MSS. :

    MS. Accounts of those deprived by Committee of Estates, 1689.
    Bp. Rattray's " Historical Account of Church of Scotland after abolition of Episcopacy ".
    " Case of Episcopal Clergy truly represented ", 1706.

ADDITIONAL BIBLIOGRAPHY
(*for the Second Edition*)

Burleigh, J. H. S., *A Church History of Scotland* (Oxford U.P. 1960).
Donaldson, Gordon, *The Scottish Reformation* (Cambridge U.P. 1960).
The Making of the Scottish Prayer Book of 1637 (Edinburgh U.P. 1954).
Scotland, Church and Nation through Sixteen Centuries (Sc. Academic Press 1972).
Scottish Historical Documents (Sc. Academic Press 1970).
Drummond and Bulloch, *The Scottish Church 1688–1843* (St. Andrew Press, Edinburgh 1973).
The Church in Victorian Scotland (Edinburgh 1975).
Fasti ecclesiae Scoticanae, *Scottish Record Society*.
Foster, W. R., *Bishop and Presbytery* (S.P.C.K. 1958).
Henderson, Ian, *Power without Glory* (1967).
Herron, Andrew, *Record Apart* (Sc. Academic Press 1974).
Highet, J., *The Churches in Scotland To-day* (1950).
Lochhead, Marion, *Episcopal Church in Scotland in the Nineteenth Century* (S.P.C.K. 1966).
Maxwell, Jean S., *A History of the Episcopal Church in Dumfries* (Dumfries 1968).
Mitchison, Rosalind, *History of Scotland* (Methuen 1970).
Moorman, J. R. H., *A History of the Church of England* (Clark 1967).
Ramsey and Suenens, *The Future of the Christian Church* (S.C.M. 1971).

REPORTS

Anglican Presbyterian Conversations, 1966.
Ecclesial Nature of the Eucharist (1973).
Intercommunion: A Scottish Episcopal Approach (R.C.C. 1969).
Multilateral Church Conversations: Interim Report, 1972 (St. Andrew Press, Edinburgh).
Partners in Mission: Report of Anglican Consultative Council (London: S.P.C.K. 1973).
Varieties of Ministry: A Report (R.C.C. 1972).

INDEX

177